The Left-hander's Handbook

The Left-hander's Handbook

Diane G Paul

First edition   1993 Dextral Books
Second edition   1998 The Robinswood Press
Reprinted 2002

British Library Cataloguing-in-Publication Data – A catalogue record for this book is available from the British Library.

The Robinswood Press

Stourbridge   England

ISBN 1 869981 59 6

www.robinswoodpress.com

CONTENTS

ACKNOWLEDGEMENTS

I would like to thank the many teachers, special educational needs providers, psychologists and parents of left-handed children who gave me the advice and support which enabled me to write this second book on left-handedness.

I am particularly grateful to Dr. Jean Alston, Audrey McAllen, Dr. Rosemary Sassoon and Prue Wallis Myers for their contributions on handwriting, to Prue Wallis Myers for many of the line drawings and to Leopard Learning for giving me permission to reproduce illustrations from Rosemary Sassoon's two books, *Handwriting: The Way to Teach it* and *Handwriting: A New Perspective*.

Diane G Paul.

*Left-handed children often draw houses with the chimney
and door handles on the left. Right-handers do the reverse.*
(Illustration by Stuart Goldwater, age 10.)

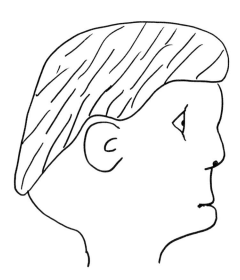

*Left-handers tend to draw profiles facing the
right. Right-handers draw them facing the left.*
(Illustration by Adam Goldwater, age 13.)

PREFACE

"Emily, the kitchen maid, made no objection to Pip stirring his tea with his knife, but what shocked her idea of etiquette and deportment was the fact that he insisted on doing so with his left hand."

Pip: a Romance of Youth.
Ian Hay, 1907.

"Dear Sir/Madam,
I am writing to you concerning my five-year-old son who, in September, will be in his second year at infant school. He is definitely left-handed. My – and his – problem is that we don't know anyone in the family or elsewhere who is left-handed. He is finding it increasingly difficult to write but, although his teachers are aware of his left-handedness, they are unable to offer any advice.

I would be most grateful for any guidance you could offer. Will he need special pens, rulers or anything else as he gets older?

From a worried mother.

Mrs C. L., Manchester."

"Dear Sir,
I am writing to you as a left-hander myself and the mother of a left-handed child. I am concerned about the lack of provision for left-handed children in our schools.

It is true that overt pressure is no longer exerted on left-handed children to use their right hand, but now the theory appears to be that left-handers should be left entirely to their own devices. It

1

seems that educationalists fail to recognise that left-handed children do have problems and that education authorities offer little or no specialist help to left-handers.

My left-handed sister, a school teacher for over 30 years, does recognise the problems and takes pains, for example, to seat left-handers on the left of double tables to avoid 'nudging' of elbows. She provides left-handed scissors and advises her left-handers on correct posture and pencil hold for writing and drawing. General guidelines on how to teach left-handed children to write correctly, however, are not provided by education authorities. Certainly, no provision is made at my teacher training college on how to teach left-handed children.

Despite being left-handed myself, I hadn't really considered these difficulties seriously until I experienced the constant complaints from my daughter's teacher about her inability to achieve both speed and neatness in her writing. I realised that I, too, have difficulty in producing fast yet neat writing. I asked the teacher if she was aware that my daughter was left-handed or if the school had a policy for teaching left-handers.

It would appear that no special tuition is given to left-handed children in the school. They are expected to cut with right-handed scissors and watch demonstrations performed in the right-handed manner only. I believe that left-handed children are left to struggle along aimlessly in the school classroom with little or no guidance.

I would be most obliged if you could advise me of any research that has been recently undertaken, and where I can obtain guides on how to teach left-handed children to write correctly.

Mrs H. H., Willenhall."

For decades, scientists worldwide have been researching laterality. Numerous scientific papers, too steeped in medical or psychological jargon to be understood by the layman, have been published in scientific journals, suggesting reasons for sinistrality, or hypothesising on its origins, its characteristics or its nature.

Individual scientists reach different conclusions on laterality, often in complete disagreement with their colleagues. Some of their theories have been replicated, with similar results, or disproved. Other theories have been left unsubstantiated. Some researchers have even contradicted or abandoned their own original theories after producing conflicting results in further experiments.

What are parents and teachers of left-handers to make of all this? And what benefit do left-handers derive from all this earnest activity on their behalf?

Little of any practical value. For the experts do not offer any valuable advice based on their findings. Neither do education authorities, on the whole, recognise left-handedness as an issue in the classroom. This is despite the persistent assertions of special educational needs teachers that there are above average percentages of left-handers in their classes. Indeed, a recent survey among special needs teachers in Berkshire revealed that the percentage of left-handed children receiving special help in Key Stage 2 was more than the total children receiving help in Key Stage 1. [1]

Out of 577 special needs children, 14.3 per cent girls and 18.2 per cent boys were left-handed. 81 per cent of the teachers themselves said left-handedness should be treated as a special issue and 85 per cent agreed that it constituted a special educational need. These teachers were more aware of left-handers' needs and were more likely to provide appropriate equipment for them than were classroom teachers.

Left-handedness is not a subject covered in teacher training colleges. Previous attempts to influence the education sector have so far come to nothing. In 1905, John Jackson founded the Society for Ambidextral Culture and Upright Writing to promote two-handed training. Among his supporters were the artist Sir Edwin Landseer and founder of the Scout Movement, Major-General Baden-Powell, both ambidextrous. 'Justice and Equality for the Left Hand' was their slogan. Some infant schools adopted the campaign and produced special copy books, but it was highly criticised by right-handers and ignored by the government.

Even today, the Department for Education and Employment holds no statistics or information on left-handed pupils. More recently, a pressure group formed by a left-handed supplier attempted to influence Parliament and the Teacher Training Agency – to no avail at the time of printing.

There have never been any official guidelines, although we have been asked for them repeatedly by trainers, teachers and parents, and the vast majority of schools have no policy for left-handers. The letters replicated above are just two of many received by the Centre for Left-Handed Studies.

The most help that is offered is confined to advising teachers to sit the left-handers on the left of double tables and provide left-handed scissors. Good sound advice, now almost a cliché, but there must surely be more words of wisdom to offer than this.

Not all left-handed children experience difficulties, but those who do are left to struggle unaided with poor handwriting skills and equipment designed for right hand use. This automatically puts them at a disadvantage at the beginning of their educational life. Bad habits and awkwardness can follow them into adulthood and affect their future careers. Job applicants are still asked to write covering letters and application forms in their own handwriting and messy, poorly written ones may influence employers' choices. Clumsy use of right-handed equipment may prove dangerous in the workplace, particularly in catering or hairdressing.

"Why should we make life easy for them? Let them try a bit harder..." a Lancashire junior school teacher said to me when she saw an exhibition of my educational items for left-handers. Other teachers and parents have begged for some guidelines on helping left-handed children. Many right-handed parents are frustrated at not being able to teach the most simple tasks to their left-handed children, like tying their shoelaces or knitting.

Teachers with large classes of children, some of whom have far more serious difficulties than a left-handed child, cannot devote the time and attention necessary to help left-handed children correct their handwriting difficulties. Most have no experience of teaching these skills to left-handers.

Primary and secondary initial teacher training aims at providing students with an introduction to the recognition of the diversity in pupils' talents and identification of their special educational needs or learning difficulties. However, left-handedness does not fall within the definition of a learning difficulty under the Education Act 1981.

Under Section 1(2), a child has a learning difficulty if he has a significantly greater difficulty in learning than the majority of other children of the same age, or a disability which prevents or hinders them from making use of educational facilities of a kind generally provided in schools. Left-handedness, therefore, has no place in either category if it stands alone. It is up to individual teachers and schools to do what they can for left-handed pupils who experience difficulties. There are, though, plenty of suppliers able to help schools to provide adequate equipment for their left-handed pupils.

A word of warning: A wealth of mythology and misinformation often surrounds left-handedness. Some people, who do not have access to current research, can sometimes become over-emotive or exaggerate the reality. It is essential for professionals with in-depth knowledge or qualifications to advise, lecture or assess such children.

A child who has visual difficulties, for example, or an inability to grasp handwriting skills may need an oculist or a handwriting consultant. Spelling, reading and writing difficulties may indicate dyslexic tendencies. Motor control difficulties may necessitate a physiotherapist or occupational therapist. A child may need an assessment on handwriting, emotional, general motor or attentional problems by an educational psychologist or a special needs teacher.

There is no proof that left-handers differ from right-handers in terms of educational attainment or IQ. They are not all geniuses or members of an elite group, any more than they are all disturbed, schizophrenic or low achievers.

This is the first published handbook for teachers and for parents and it provides practical suggestions for helping left-handed children master tasks which might otherwise put some of them at a disadvantage during the early stages of their education. It has been compiled with the help of special educational needs experts, psychologists, class teachers, head teachers and handwriting consultants, experts who understand the needs of left-handed children.

The first edition of this book won a British Medical Association Book Award in 1995. This second edition expands on some of the previous information and up-dates references. The special *Guidelines* at the end of most Chapters have now been adopted as research-based practical educational resource packs by the National Foundation for Educational Research in the U.K. and the New Zealand Council for Educational Research. It can only be hoped that it will help to dispense with some of the mythology surrounding left-handedness and become a bookshelf classic for teachers and parents who seek positive ways of helping left-handed children.

Diane G Paul.
Manchester, 1998.

Footnote:

1   Bentley, D., and R. Stainthorp. *The Needs of the Left-Handed Child in the Infant Classroom – Writing is Not Always Right* (UKRA, 1992).

INTRODUCTION

In 1992, the Centre for Left-Handed Studies (CLHS – now defunct), conducted a research project in eight Greater Manchester junior schools, funded by the Calouste Gulbenkian Foundation.

Of 1,060 7-11 year-olds surveyed, 11 per cent were found to be non-right-handed, or at least to use their left hand for writing. Although teachers report larger incidences of left-handedness in their classes nowadays, possibly resulting from a more liberal policy towards them than in previous generations, the percentages do not reflect this as they have not increased significantly over time.

Left-handed girls accounted for nine per cent of the sample and left-handed boys for 12 per cent, which was also in line with traditional estimates. [1]

The results of this survey also revealed, paradoxically, that although 79 per cent of the 71 teachers questioned claimed they 'made efforts to help left-handers', 70 per cent believed that 'left-handers were not educationally disadvantaged', and only 63 per cent were 'aware of the individual left-handed pupils in their care'.

It would be gratifying to find that 100 per cent of teachers were aware of their left-handed pupils, and 100 per cent made a conscious effort to help those who needed it. But first, we would have to see the adoption of guidelines which are instituted from teacher training level onwards and a universal policy for left-handers in schools.

Only 17 per cent of parents provided left-handers with special scissors. Many did not know these existed. In some classes, left-handed scissors were available, but were not being distributed. When teaching handwriting, only 1 in 12 teachers helped with letter construction, only 1 in 18 with book placement, and just 1 in 35 with correct pencil hold.

Left-handers experienced the most everyday difficulties using right-handed potato peelers, knitting and sewing, handling cutlery and using scissors. Twice as many left-handers as right-handers found it difficult to tie shoelaces, or use knives or pens, and the same proportion suffered from left : right confusion.

The boys showed more educational difficulties than the girls. Left-handers were observed by their teachers to have lower reading ability, poorer hand-eye co-ordination and mixed disabilities.

Although many dyslexics are also left-handed, none was noted, until a handwriting test revealed several who showed dyslexic characteristics and who were obviously being overlooked.

A handwriting test revealed a sub-group of fast writers among the left-handers who were good spellers and highly creative. Although the majority of left-handers showed little difference in performance to the right-handers, there was a second sub-group at the opposite extreme, who performed particularly poorly.

It was conjectured that the first group may have comprised genetic, or natural, left-handers who performed inordinately well and the second group, pathological, or forced left-handers, who were inordinately weak. Left-handers were superior to right-handers in music.

The results of the survey revealed clearly that there were no standard systems for aiding left-handers with difficulties and that despite denials from some quarters, the statistics showed that left-handers appear to have more difficulties in the classroom than right-handers at the junior school level. It is true that they have more difficulties working with everyday items designed specifically for right-handers.

It has not been my intention to produce a catalogue of negative traits displayed by left-handers. On the contrary, some of the world's greatest achievers, whose names will never be forgotten, have been left-handed: Sir Paul McCartney, Albert Einstein, Pablo Picasso, Marilyn Monroe, Sir Charles Chaplin, Martina Navratilova, John McEnroe, Greta Garbo, and 30 per cent of all the Presidents of the United States, including President Clinton. All three candidates for

President of the U.S.A. in 1992 were left-handers. Even President Reagan was a left-hander who had suffered an enforced change to right-handedness. Leonardo da Vinci and Michelangelo were said to be left-handed and were certainly strongly ambidextrous.

Nor do I suggest that left-handers should develop militant tendencies and litigate: like the American checkout cashier who sued her firm successfully for $136,700 when they changed to computerised systems which she was unable to operate; or the 12-year-old Viennese boy who decided to sue his parents for the 'years of difficulty and hardship' he had undergone as a left-hander, claiming that his schoolwork had suffered and he had had a tough time at games. He blamed his divorced parents, both of whom were left-handers.

What should be discouraged is the growing fashion for some left-handers to either exaggerate their difficulties, real or imagined, or to elevate left-handers as an élitist band of superior beings. Neither is accurate, for adult left-handers, and many young left-handers too, manage perfectly well in a right-handed world. Nor are they, as a group, any more privileged than their right-handed counterparts.

The aim of this guide is, rather, to identify any key problem areas and suggest practical solutions and working methods to ease the burden faced by those young left-handers at home and in the classroom for whom, until now, there has been no official support. Their needs are different from those of right-handers and there is no reason why they should struggle unaided, when a simple policy for left-handers could be introduced in schools.

Footnote:

1   While handedness statistics vary, no left-handed culture has ever been found. The highest percentage of left-handers noted in any culture has been among the Kwakiutl Indians of British Columbia, of whom 17-22 per cent are left-handed or ambidextrous for writing. Interestingly, the Manchester survey noted that 17 per cent of pupils in a Jewish school were left-handed. This was confirmed in three other schools and from later enquiries in other cities. Lack of funding has prevented any further research into genetic links.

1 DEFINITIONS

Much of the information written about left-handedness is taken from research documents, many of which are difficult to translate into plain language for the layman. Some terms are not easily understood. People are inclined to boast about their 'ambidexterity' when what they really mean is that they are mixed-handed. It is quite rare to find an ambidextrous person, for few of them exist.

I am providing a glossary at the beginning so that some of the terms used in this book can be clearly understood from the start.

Ambidextrous (ambidexterity)
Able to use both hands equally well for all tasks. To have no actual preference for either hand. Can be left- or right-handed at will. Surgeons need this facility, decorators could do with it and Leonardo da Vinci, Michelangelo and Queen Victoria had it, the former more by design than by nature. Many Renaissance artists were encouraged to develop ambidexterity. Once encouraged in schools by John Jackson, founder of the Society for Ambidextral Culture and Upright Writing, but it floundered – as did the Society.

Ambiguous-handed
No consistent hand preference formed. Hand use changes between and during performance of tasks. Undetermined-handedness.

Ambilateral
Not skilful with either hand.

Attention Deficit Disorder and
Attention Deficit Hyperactivity Disorder
The cause of developmental learning disorders and formerly referred to as Minimal Brain Dysfunction. (For symptoms, see Chapter 4.) Caused by deficient levels of neuro-transmitter substances in brain cells and occurs mostly in boys. ADD sufferers

are mainly overactive but some are underactive. ADD cannot be cured but it can be alleviated. Often, ADD adults are high achievers, although some display social problems. They are usually cross-lateral, displaying mixed-handedness, and a lack of fixed dominance. May be left-handed but have right eye or right foot preference. This trait is additional to any learning disorders, not the cause.

Bi-manual
Carrying out different tasks or actions using both hands simultaneously.

Cerebral hemispheres
The two halves of the brain.

Cerebral lateralisation
The complementary relationship between the brain's two hemispheres. Linked to handedness.

Corpus Callosum
Millions of nerve fibres which link the cerebral hemispheres and transmit messages to and from them.

Crossed-laterality
A mixture of sidedness, such as left-handed but right-footed and right-eyed. This can cause some co-ordination problems. Crossed hand/eye dominance can affect performance in some sports, such as racquet sports where the field of vision might sometimes be restricted. It can be advantageous in gymnastics, running and netball, because positioning of the body would be more evenly distributed for better balance.

Degree
A range of handedness from strong to weak left to weak to strong right. Weak right-handers are often included with 'non-right-handers', creating confusion in the results of research studies and handedness questionnaires. An official census of left-handers would present an inaccurate picture because of the difficulty in defining left-handedness as such. (See also: direction.)

Dexterity
Skill in using the hands. Also dextrous.

Dextral(ity)
The terms used for right-handers and right-handedness, specific to human beings.

Digital manipulation
Flexing the fingers and thumb into the hand and releasing them out.

Direction
As opposed to degree of handedness. Concerns right versus left only. The implications are different for direction and degree. The latter has been little researched.

Dyslexia
Difficulty in learning to read, write or spell correctly and express thoughts on paper. Between 15 and 75 per cent of dyslexics noted at the beginning of the century were left-handed. It was suggested that all dyslexic children should become left-handers. As with left-handedness, numerous theories were suggested for its origins by educational psychologists, most of them spurious. Known by various terms, such as 'congenital word-blindness', 'strepho-symbolia' (twisted symbols), 'specific dyslexia', 'developmental dyslexia', 'specific learning difficulty' and 'reading retardation'. Controversy rages over how to define a dyslexic, but generally people whose reading ability does not measure up to their IQ.

Ear preference
The ear, like the eye, is not linked to laterality, being a sensory not a motor organ. Most people are, in fact, right-eared, which may indicate a link to left hemisphere language processing.

Eye preference
Confusion in terms can arise between the dominant eye, the preferred eye, and the leading eye. The eye which has the better sight is not always the preferred or dominant one. The latter may be the weaker one, which could present reading difficulties. No dominance occurs when both eyes are used. The preferred eye is a matter of choice when using one eye, for example, for a telescope or microscope. The incidence of left-eye dominance varies between 25 and 35 per cent with about a third of the population showing some sort of preference for the left. It is not necessarily linked to left-handedness.

Foot preference
Although the foot is not used for the same manipulative functions as the hand, it is still a motor function and is considered to be linked to handedness. The dominant foot, furthermore, is not vulnerable to influence of training, unlike the hand, and is therefore a constant indicator of laterality preference.

Hand preference
The preferred hand for certain tasks, which is usually chosen for its proficiency. If both hands are equally proficient, then either hand would be chosen as the preferred hand. However, if one hand is more proficient than the other, that usually becomes the preferred hand.

Hand proficiency
The most skilful hand at certain tasks.

Handedness
The tendency towards the predominant use of a preferred hand, classified by the writing hand or the hand most used for a range of activities.

Lateral asymmetry
The different functions or specialisations of the cerebral hemispheres.

Laterality
Sidedness – left and right sides, distinct from preference.

Mirror writing
Letters and words written by the left hand from right to left of the page and formed in reverse. Can be read correctly only when reflected in a mirror. (Leonardo da Vinci, Samuel Pepys and Lewis Carroll were able to do this at will, the latter purely for enjoyment.) Because the tendency is to push the pen away from the body, young left-handers will often begin writing this way. As some children can also read backwards with ease, they may not be aware at first that they are doing anything out of the ordinary. (See Chapter 7 for solutions.) Some right-handed children also do this until corrected. Some people are able to do this with both hands simultaneously. ('Cheats' stick a piece of paper under the desk or on their forehead and write normally. When removed, the paper contains perfect mirror writing.)

Right-handers should be able to mirror write in Hebrew, which is written from right to left and would be more natural for a left-hander to follow. It is also easier to write backwards than forwards with the left foot.

An example of mirror writing by the author.

Mixed-handedness
Using either hand for different tasks. Most left-handers are mixed-handed.

Non-right-handedness
Not necessarily left-handedness, but refers to any consistent deviation from right-handedness. Constitutes a range of functional differences displayed by left- or mixed-handers. Can include strong and weak left-handers and weak right-handers (the latter more numerous than the other two groups). Confusion occurs in research when it becomes unclear whether direction (left or right) or degree of handedness (strong or weak) is under scrutiny. [1] Researchers tend to use non-right-handedness as the criteria for research, which puts the incidence for what is commonly termed left-handedness at eight per cent of the population.

Sidedness
The difference between left and right sides.

Sinistral(ity)
The terms used for left-handers and left-handedness. Sinister is the Latin word for left and denotes bad luck and everything perverse. In Anglo-Saxon, 'lyft' means weak or broken.

Speech lateralisation
The cerebral hemisphere which is specialised for the use of language. This is usually the left hemisphere but for non-right-handers, 70 per cent in the left hemisphere, 15 per cent in the right hemisphere and 15 per cent across both hemispheres.

Tests

Tests for hand, foot, ear and eye preference can be found on pages 103 to 108.

Undetermined-handedness

See Ambiguous-handedness.

Uni-manual

Carrying out tasks or actions with one hand only.

Footnote:

1   McManus, I. C. *The Interpretation of Laterality* (*Cortex*, 19, 1983). Pages 187-214.

2 FREQUENTLY ASKED QUESTIONS

"My baby keeps reaching for things with
his left hand. Is he going to be left-handed?"

Most babies use both hands initially and no preference is usually apparent until between seven and nine months of age. Direction of hand preference should become consistent after about 18 months. Even then, preference may not be established until the child is around three years old, when a more defined pattern may be observed.

Degree of hand preference continues developing until at least nine years of age. Children who draw with the left hand but throw, catch and bounce a ball with the right hand have not established their dominance.

Researchers have also noted a tendency for babies to turn their heads to one side while lying on their backs, which they maintain indicates lateralisation preferences (assymetric tonic neck reflex). Babies with a right head-turning bias have been found to grow up as right-handers but the left head-turners show no particular hand preference, indicating that they may grow up more mixed-sided. [1]

Babies tend to change hands at different stages of their development. The charts on the following page illustrate a natural pattern of hand changes noted among babies and young children over periods of time.

It was also found that boys tend to lateralise earlier than girls. Early lateralisers are generally strong left-handers.

AGE OF LATERALISATION

Weeks	Hands
12	Both.
16 - 20	Left.
24	Both.
28	Right.
32	Both.
36	Left.
40 - 44	Right.
48	Left.
52 - 56	Right.
80	Both.

Years	Hands
2	Right.
$2^1/_2$ - $3^1/_2$	Both.
4	Dominance shows.
8	Dominance established.

"Is it true that left-handers are more intelligent than right-handers?"

In terms of mental ability and educational attainment, researchers have consistently not found any significant difference between left- and right-handers generally, although there appears to be little relationship between handedness and mental testing. However, questionnaires completed by school teachers, who have direct knowledge of their pupils' classroom performances, often reveal a different picture to that of individual testing, showing lower levels of achievement by left-handers in the 7-11 age group. In handwriting tests, sub-groups of left-handers performed either very poorly or inordinately well. [2]

Scientists do not regard observation as a yardstick for measuring accurate scientific data, but one has to consider that not only have their own methods produced consistently conflicting results, but that a child's performance under test conditions may differ markedly from that displayed unselfconsciously and habitually in the classroom.

"Newspaper articles sometimes suggest that left-handers are more accident prone than right-handers, and even live shorter lives. What is the truth behind such reports?"

Researchers in Canada produced statistics taken a) from an American baseball encyclopaedia and b) from relatives of people who had died six months before. [3] The research has been refuted in America [4] and replicated with statistics from a cricket encyclopaedia in England. [5]

The results are not representative of the population at large as no women were included, only left-handed bowlers in both cases. World-class slow bowler, Robert ('Bobby') Peel (1857-1941) died aged 84, although he was known to be accident prone.

Their deduction that left-handers suffer more accidents from utensils designed for right-handers and that they were more likely to die in battle because of right-handed weaponry, may well be accurate. A dearth of older left-handers can be accounted for by the fact that most would have suffered enforced changes to right-handedness by parents or teachers.

However, only a true study of longevity, monitoring a right and a left-handed group through their lifespan would produce accurate results, and this has never been undertaken. It may also be worth noting that left-handers Sir Rex Harrison died aged 82, Sir Charles Chaplin at 78, and Greta Garbo, at the age of 85.

This is rather an extreme term and its use alarms people unnecessarily. Some strongly left- or mixed-handers may have had damaged left hemispheres pre- or peri-natally, without which they would probably have been born right-handed, but they are not 'brain damaged' as such. (See Chapter 3, pathological left-handers.) However, there are found to be higher than average percentages of non-right-handers among certain neurologically-damaged children, cerebral palsy sufferers, for example. Language lateralisation may also be affected.

A lack of hand preference (ambiguous handedness), as opposed to actual left-handedness, has been noted among higher than normal percentages of autistic, mentally handicapped and Down's Syndrome children, although it is not clear whether this is due to pathological causes or dysfunction of motor skills. High percentages of non-right-handers have been noted among epileptics who had early left hemisphere damage, but such damage occurring at a later age does not appear to affect a child's right-handedness.

Non-pathological left-handers are classed as genetic (natural) left-handers, but it is difficult to distinguish genetic from pathological left-handers, especially where there are no signs of brain damage.

*"If a left-handed child is forced to write
with the right hand, can a stutter develop?"*

Stuttering was often reported in children who were forcibly changed to right-handedness – for example, King George VI. Right-handers and 70 per cent of non-right-handers have speech in their left hemisphere. Half of the rest have speech in the right hemisphere and half have it spread across both hemispheres. Much of the early research showed high percentages of changed non-right-handers with stutters. It was thought that an enforced change to right-handedness interfered with speech. Certainly, many older left-handed people I have spoken to report a period of stuttering after they were forced to write with their right hand. From the 1940s, this theory began to wane in popularity, subsequent researchers preferring to believe the stress of the change created the speech defect, and others that there was no connection between enforced change and stuttering at all.

Even so, it is unwise to force a non-right-hander into right-handedness. High percentages of non-right-handers, dyslexics and ADD children suffer from short-term memory difficulties. Stuttering can occur when trying to verbalise an idea that has been formed, because the short-term memory prevents the child from remembering back to the beginning. Verbalisation is then punctuated by hesitation and confusion.

"Left-handers seem to have an advantage in sports where quick reactions are crucial. Is this because they have very good spatial awareness?"

As usual there is some disagreement about this among researchers. In 1981, 20 per cent of top tennis professionals were left-handed. In the 1990s left-handed male professionals accounted for 19 per cent of the total. (In actual fact, the U.K.'s Ann Jones is the only left-handed female tennis player to win Wimbledon's Ladies' Singles Championship besides Martina Navratilova – 9 times winner – beating Billie-Jean King in 1969. She also won the mixed doubles title.)

A third of top fencers are left-handed. Left-handers are also well represented in professional cricket, table tennis and baseball. In 1980, six of the world championship top ten table tennis players were left-handers.

Some studies suggest that left-handers have quicker reflex reactions because the right side of the brain handles visual information and orders the appropriate motor response. In truth, they probably have a tactical advantage in that they most likely put off their right-handed opponents in face-to-face play. Right-handers are generally inexperienced at playing against left-handers and in tennis, for example, are used to placing the ball in different areas of the court to gain the advantage over right-handed players. The left-hander's serve is also difficult to return.

The only sports banned to left hand play are polo and hockey where a left-hander would be playing against the rest of the field. Although no left-handed hockey sticks exist, players can play on the left on the reverse stick side. Tactics include a scoop from the left, the jab, the left hand wing, reverse stick stops and dribbling. Left-handed goalies are at an advantage as most penalties are aimed at the non-stick (left) side where their reactions are fastest. In athletics, the javelin has right hand grips and throwing a discus or hammer is dangerous when thrown by a left-hander. But football players on the left wing or full back are advantaged when kicking towards the centre.

"Are left-handers more creative and artistic than right-handers?"

A   Left-handed artists are often thought to have particularly high spatial awareness – Michelangelo and Leonardo da Vinci being quoted amongst the most famous. Both, of course, were members of the Renaissance school of artists that encouraged the use of both hands. In one study of art students, 21 per cent were left-handed and 28 per cent mixed-handed. [6] However, other studies contradict these findings and similar theories concerning left-handed architects. The fact remains, though, that architects frequently report high numbers of left-handers among their ranks.

*"Now that left-handedness is no longer stopped,
has the incidence risen and what is it now?"*

The measured incidence of left-handedness has always varied among researchers. Teachers report noticing more of them in their classes these days. Because left-handers cannot be classified in one homogeneous group, they are generally categorised by writing hands. The Scottish Council for Research in Education reported an increase among ten-year-olds from 6.8 per cent boys and 5.1 per cent girls in 1963 to 8.2 per cent boys and 6.7 per cent girls in 1968. [7]

Educational psychologist, Margaret Clark, reported 8.8 per cent left-handed writers among seven-year-olds in 1970. [8] There have always been more left-handed boys than girls noted. In the U.S.A. in 1962, of 92,656 children surveyed, 11.1 per cent boys and 9.7 per cent girls were left-handed writers. [9] A meta-analysis of 88 previous research studies put the incidence at 7.78 per cent in 1990. [10]

Researchers generally claim the incidence as around eight per cent of the population from their own tests, although often their criteria for left-handedness is based on more than just the writing hand. For this reason, a general census would not give a true result. They also claim no increase in the incidence for five millennia, which they deduce from art historical evidence. [11]

However, the subjects of primitive wall paintings can hardly be classified as an indication of left-handedness – many of the figures depicted with weapons or tools in their right hands may simply have been illustrated that way by artistic whim, or to avoid obstructing the foreground. Left-handed illustrations face to the right, right-handed to the left. This again would only indicate the frequency of left-handed drawings. Given the stringency with which scientists test and re-test on handedness questionnaires it seems out of keeping with their usual approach.

Nevertheless, recent surveys in Berkshire and Manchester LEA schools indicate incidences of 11 and 13 per cent respectively, although these were confined to left-handed writers. [2]

Footnotes:

1 Coryell, J. F. and G. F. Michel. *How supine postural preferences of infants can contribute toward the development of handedness* (Infant Behavior and Development, 1, 1978). Pages 245-257.

2 Paul, D. *Laterality Study in Manchester Junior Schools* (Manchester: Centre for Left-Handed Studies, 1992). Research project funded by the Calouste Gulbenkian Foundation.

   Bentley, D. and R. Stainthorp. *The Needs of the Left-Handed Child in the Infant Classroom – Writing is Not Always Right* (UKRA, 1992).

3 Coren, S. *The Left-Hander Syndrome: The Causes and Consequences of Left-Handedness* (London: John Murray, 1992).

   Coren, S. and D. F. Halpern. *Left-handedness: a marker for decreased survival fitness* (Psychological Bulletin, 109, 1992). Pages 90-106.

   Halpern, D. F. and S. Coren. *Do right-handers live longer?* (Nature, 333, 213, 1988).

   Coren, S. *Left-handedness and accident-related injury risk* (American Journal of Public Health, 79, 1-2, 1989).

   Halpern D. F. and S. Coren. *Handedness and life span* (New England Journal of Medicine, 1991). Pages 324 and 998.

4 National Institutes of Health and Harvard University study (1993).

5 Aggleton, J. P., R. W. Kentridge and N. J. Neave. *Evidence for longevity differences between left-handed and right-handed men: an archival study of cricketers* (Journal of Epidemiology and Community Health, 47, 1993). Pages 206-209.

6 Mebert, C. J. and G. F. Michel. *Handedness in artists* in: Herron, J. (Ed.) *The Neuropsychology of Left-handedness* (New York: Academic Press, 1980). Pages 273-279.

7 Scottish Council for Research in Education. *The Scottish Scholastic Survey - 1953* (London: University of London Press, 1963).

8 Clark, M. *Reading Difficulties in Schools* (Harmondsworth: Penguin, 1970).

9 Enstrom, E. A. *The extent of the use of the left hand in handwriting* (Journal of Educational Research, 55, v, 1962). Pages 234-5.

10 Seddon, B. M. and I. C. McManus. *The inheritance of left-handedness: A meta-analysis* (1991).

11 Coren, S. and C. Porac. *Fifty centuries of right-handedness: the historical record* (Science, 198, 1977). Pages 631-632.

3 CAUSES OF LEFT-HANDEDNESS

Defining Left-handedness

For the purposes of this book, we will define left-handers as children who write with their left hands, although some left-handed children may divide other tasks between hands (mixed-handers) or even change hands whilst carrying out the same tasks (ambiguous-handers).

Researchers tend to classify left-handers by three criteria:

1) Is the left hand used for writing?

2) Is it the hand preferred for certain key tasks, used consistently? (Measured either by handedness questionnaires or by carrying out a range of uni-manual performance tasks.)

3) Is it the most skilful, proficient or most able hand? (Measured by manual tasks using one hand, followed by the other, for example, moving pegs across a board.)

Many famous 'left-handed' sportsmen are actually not left-handed at all. Two-handed actions, like sweeping and batting, are often carried out by right-handers with their left hands, and vice versa. Both ace cricketer David Gower and champion golfer Bob Charles are right-handers, yet they play on the left while carrying out single-handed actions with their right hands, for example, writing and throwing.

The suggested causes of left-handedness have already been covered in *Living Left-Handed* (Bloomsbury Publishing Ltd., 1997). The intention here is to provide some practical tips to make life easier for left-handed children, not to replicate material available elsewhere.

Despite this, it is important to be aware that there are varying degrees of left-handedness and that, while most left-handers will experience no difficulties or, at worst, only minor ones, there are others who will need special help.

The Brain

George Bush declared the 1990s the 'Decade of the Brain'. Advances in technology have furthered our understanding of the way the brain works and opened up new ways of thinking quite dramatically. More is now known about the brain than ever before. Despite this, the left-handed mythology persists:

"...the right brain is the intuitive, visual side, controlling non-verbal memory, emotions, and concrete thinking. The left brain is the logical, verbal side, controlling speech, writing and abstract thinking. Due to their right brain dominance, left-handers are therefore intuitive, emotional, creative, illogical, musical, have high spatial awareness and relate well to concrete concepts. Some are geniuses. Left-handers are the artists and right-handers the thinkers..."

Although scientists have long since consigned such claims to the laterality dustbin where they doubtless belong, it has not stopped the media and left-handed groups perpetuating this mythology. Furthermore, despite these positive attributes, we are assured by the same people that tens of thousands of left-handers are languishing at school where they lag behind their right-handed peers, without a hope for the future. Although handedness and cerebral lateralisation are not altogether unrelated, such blanket classifications basically belong to the realm of pop psychology.

The Two Hemispheres

The brain is divided into two halves, the right and left hemispheres. Although they look symmetrical, resembling two halves of a walnut, in action they are not, as they carry out different functions. Messages are passed between them by bundles of around 200 million nerve fibres, known as the Corpus Callosum. The left hemisphere controls the right side of the body and the right hemisphere controls the left side of the body.

The notion that each hemisphere contained specific characteristics began in the early 19th Century and led to the birth of phrenology, a pseudo-science. It set off the thought among scientists that certain areas might be responsible for controlling behaviour. Around 1836, research on patients who had suffered speech loss and left hemisphere damage led to the theory that both hemispheres carried out different functions and that speech was contained in the left hemisphere.

It was 1861 before the research of neurosurgeon, Paul Broca, confirmed these findings. It was Broca who found a link between left hemisphere speech and right-handedness, assuming incorrectly that left-handers would simply be a mirror image with speech in the right hemisphere. [1]

Unfortunately, this is one of the myths that survives to this day. We now know that around 70 per cent of left-handers are no different to right-handers and that the rest have speech either in the right hemisphere or spread across both hemispheres.

Broca's Area, a small area at the left front of the brain, deals with the organisation and production of speech. If damaged, the patient would be unable to speak, but would still comprehend other people's speech, indicating that this was only one speech area. [2] It was Karl Wernicke who discovered Wernicke's Area, further back in the left hemisphere, which, when damaged, resulted in gibberish and the lack of comprehension of others' speech.

Not long afterwards, the dominant hemisphere theory was accepted, with the left side the major player and the right, the minor. The latter was largely ignored until 1876, when the British neurologist, John Hughlings Jackson, identified the right hemisphere as dominant for visual concepts. [3] In the 1930s, researchers attributed spatial and perceptual thinking areas to the right brain. [4]

It was not until the split brain operations on epileptic patients in the 1950s, when the Corpus Callosum and smaller links (commissures) were cut to relieve seizures, that the hemispheres could be tested individually and the spatial awareness of the right hemisphere confirmed.

Although research has consigned language to the left and spatial abilities, music and emotional processing to the right hemispheres, it is this sort of over-simplification that has created much of the misinformation. It must be remembered that the two hemispheres are actually interconnected. For example, although musical ability, pitch and intonation are right brain functions, note recognition, complex rhythm and the more theoretical aspects of music are functions of the left brain. It is hard for one to exist without the other.

It is dangerous, then, for left-handers to claim the attributes of right brain dominance when we know that both hemispheres continually communicate with one another, that their functions overlap and that the right hemisphere passes messages to the left hemisphere which converts them into language.

The Right Brain

We are living in an age when the current search for self-fulfilment and inner peace has heralded a wave of New Age-type philosophies promoting holistic 'right brain thinking'. Our education system has been blamed for its over-emphasis on left-brain learning. People are characterised as left or right-brained, according to their personalities.

But they can be trained to learn right brain techniques which will improve their problem-solving, creative and artistic abilities. Books, tapes and workshops abound on the theory. Techniques suggested include reading, listening to music, relaxation, changing from right to left hand activity – no instructions here as to what benefit a left-hander would derive from changing to right-hand activity.

If these philosophies differ markedly from those of the scientists who produce the data on brain characteristics and functions, it is because the true findings have been distorted en route to the general public by the reporting process and further distorted on repetition elsewhere, leaving the neuropsychologist who made the discoveries well out of the equation. The gossip becomes rumour, and the rumour becomes mythology which in turn, becomes the accepted truth.

Educational psychologists, Haydyck and Haapenen, writing about research on hemisphere specialisation, warn that there is *"no scientific basis... for any reorganisation of curricular, teaching or testing programs within contemporary educational practice."* [5] But people only believe what they want to believe and there is money to be made out of the right brain technique hype.

Canadian psychologist, Professor Stanley Coren, puts what he terms the Two-Minds Theory into its logical perspective when he states that *"...people will tend to select an occupation consistent with their cognitive style."* But higher than average percentages of left-handers have been found in research among artists, architects and chess players, who require good spatial skills. Coren points out that the differences between right and left-handers in these areas are small. There are many more famous right-handed artists and many successful left-handed writers. Coren writes *"The ability of handedness to predict thinking style or specific areas of ability is at best weak and only suggestive."* [6]

As for musicians, where high percentages of left and mixed-handers are noted, Coren states that it is only in pitch recognition where left-handers are advantaged. Left-handers show no superior creative abilities when tested, which suggests that handedness and creativity are not linked.

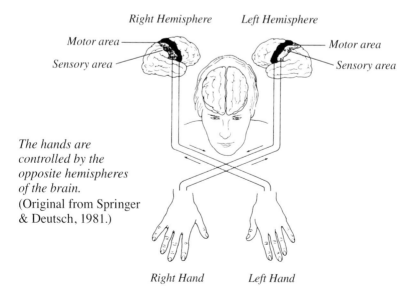

Right Hemisphere   *Left Hemisphere*

Motor area ———   ——— *Motor area*
Sensory area ———   ——— *Sensory area*

The hands are controlled by the opposite hemispheres of the brain.
(Original from Springer & Deutsch, 1981.)

Right Hand   *Left Hand*

Causes of Left-handedness

It is generally accepted by scientists that right-handedness is a genetic characteristic of human beings. People who are strongly and consistently right-handed come under this classification. Any deviation from this norm is classified as non-right-handedness. Because high incidences of left-handedness were found among afflicted groups, such as epileptics, schizophrenics and the like, it was originally thought that the cause of left-handedness was pathological, which involved some damage to the brain in utero, during or after birth.

Most left-handers show no signs of pathology and perform perfectly well, excelling in many areas. This led researchers to believe that there were two main types of left-handers, those with a pathology and those who were natural genetic left-handers.

Pathological (Forced) Left-handers

Some researchers believe that the left hemisphere develops last, exposing it for a longer period of time to anything which may affect the brain, although other researchers disagree. Some left-handers would have been right-handed but for some injury to the left hemisphere which induced them to change to the non-affected side. Often, they experience additional problems, which is why we hear about higher than average percentages of non-right-handers (left- and mixed-handers) among dyslexics, children with Attention Deficit Disorder and other learning disabilities. Others may show minor, or no obvious evidence of impairment.

One of the causes of such damage has been attributed to an excess of the male hormone, testosterone, passed by the mother to the foetus, restricting growth of the left hemisphere. As slightly more males are inclined to be non-right-handers than females, some scientists believe that an excess of testosterone may be one of the reasons for this; the male foetus makes its own testosterone in addition to any absorbed from the pregnant mother. Links were found between left-handedness and immune disorders. [7] Other scientists believe that slow maturation may account for non-right-handedness, and males mature more slowly than females.

Some research has shown that low weight or premature babies, and birth stress accounts for left- or mixed-handed children. Canadian psychologist, Stanley Coren, categorises his research findings in this field to include: premature birth; prolonged labour; breathing difficulties caused by lack of oxygen; low birth weight (below six pounds); breech birth; RH incompatibility, where a mother with a Rhesus plus antigen gives birth to a baby with a Rhesus negative antigen, or vice versa; instrument birth, where forceps may be used on the baby during delivery; Caesarean births and multiple births. Another finding was that older mothers were more likely to suffer from birth complications and so produce non-right-handed offspring. [6] Norwegian researchers have found that routine ultrasonography carried out on pregnant mothers produced a high percentage of non-right-handers, [8] as do mothers who smoke. [9]

It is difficult to determine whether or not a child is a pathological left-hander because there may well be other left-handers in the family, which might suggest a genetic bias. Conversely, some genetic left-handers may have no left-handers in the immediate family and assume incorrectly that the child is pathologically left-handed.

Pathological left-handedness does not always reflect neurological impairment. Dorothy Bishop estimates that one in 20 left-handers, and just over a third of left-handers with very poor non-preferred hand skills, can be classified as pathological left-handers. [10]

Some markers which may indicate a pathological left-hander:
1) Very early, strong lateralisation.
2) Restriction of growth in one hand or foot.
3) Very poor right hand skills.

Genetic (Natural) Left-handers

Until now, no gene for handedness per se has been identified, although recent research at the Baylor College of Medicine, Houston has led to the discovery of a laterality gene which distinguishes left from right in mice. This may, in turn, lead to the discovery of a specific gene for handedness in humans.

Animals tend to be ambidextrous, showing inconsistencies in paw preference in the main. Preference for the right hand appears to be a specifically human trait. Annett's Right Shift Factor theory proposes that handedness is determined mainly by chance with a selective advantage to the right hand, hand preference being largely a measure of skill. Consequently, people who are more skilful with their right hands will be right-handed and vice versa for left-handers.

The strength or degree of their handedness depends on the amount of difference in skill between both hands. People with little difference in skill are more likely to show right hand preference owing to cultural influences. This Right Shift Factor is inherited, a double or single dose of the two alleles [11] identified indicating the strength of right-handedness.

People whose handedness is determined by chance lack one allele (rs-) and do not possess the Right Shift Factor. Those who possess the other (rs+), in a single or double dose, will show a preference for the right side. Most left-handers are rs--, and show no genetic bias to a particular side. Cerebral lateralisation and handedness for people with no Right Shift Factor is therefore a matter of chance. The two are not connected.

Those with the Right Shift Factor will always have speech in the left hemisphere unless brain damage has occurred. To put it simply, it is a gene for speech in the left hemisphere which accompanies right-sidedness. A weak or missing gene can produce a left- or a right-hander by chance. [12] Finding a gene for handedness and cerebral dominance would unlock the neuro-biology of language. [13]

In terms of degree, research shows that it is the strongly left- and right-handers who are at risk from learning difficulties, the nearer to left of centre on the continuum proving the most beneficial. Consequently, it is no good thing to be too right-handed!

Where both parents or the mother are left-handed, there is a higher chance that there will be left-handers in the family. Left-handed mothers are more likely to have left-handed children than left-handed fathers. This could be genetic or a socially influenced effect. Adopted children do not seem to pick up the laterality preferences of their adoptive parents.

Two right-handed parents will produce around 9 per cent left-handed children, two left-handed parents, around 26 per cent and one left and one right-handed parent around 19 per cent. [14]

Social Influences and Cultural Pressures

Stories of forced hand change are rare nowadays, but they still occur, including one instance revealed in the CLHS report (not from any of the schools surveyed). Children should never be forcibly changed.

Many left-handed children carry out tasks with their right hands because they are taught that way, for example, hitting with a bat or racquet or playing a musical instrument. Many utensils and instruments are so designed that they have no option but to use their right hands, which in time becomes a habit, however awkwardly they may perform.

Perhaps there is no bad thing in using both hands. Perhaps it would cause more confusion. Renaissance artists were encouraged to use both hands, for example Michelangelo and Leonardo da Vinci. (The latter is said to have been a changed right-hander, due to an accident.) Whatever the true situation, left-handers are certainly more versatile than right-handers in their adaptation to a world designed for the latter.

If left-handed children find it too confusing or difficult to use their right hands for certain tasks, it is always best to let them use their preferred hands. Choice of the left hand does not always reflect proficiency of that hand, but often indicates a weakness in the right hand, consequently many so-called left-handers are really weak right-handers.

Some left-handers come under the influence of right-handed parents, teachers, siblings and friends. Thinking they are doing something wrong, they may copy them with the right hand. Equally, some right-handed children, whose parents or teachers are left-handed, may use their left hands for some tasks, so inevitably some social influences are bound to contribute to a child's choice of hands.

GUIDELINES **1**

1) Never force a left-hander to use the right hand. If you find it difficult to demonstrate the left-handed way, or if the child would be at a disadvantage carrying out a task with the left hand, try teaching the right-handed way at first, gently. If this proves impossible, do not pursue this.

2) Teachers and parents should be aware of the left-handers in their care. Schools are advised to record left-handers at reception level and monitor them as they rise through the school.

3) Be aware of the different types of left-handers. For those who experience difficulties, two types of problem may occur:

   a) Difficulty using equipment designed for right-hand use. Left-handers may be clumsy or accident prone. Look out for items which may prove dangerous, such as controls or leads on the right side which can be tripped over, become entangled or pull equipment off surfaces if they lie in the wrong direction for a left-hander; positioning of equipment, especially in laboratories, workbenches, and kitchens. With computer stations, remember to place mouse on left side.

   b) Possible difference in processing information. Left-handers may take longer to assimilate facts (although they often catch up and overtake their right-handed peers later) and may use a more circuitous route to arrive at the answer. Some also take longer to write, especially during examinations, because of poor paper position or penhold and because they may need to lift their arm frequently to see what they are writing.

4) Do not assume your left-handers are lazy, not trying hard enough, 'thick' or 'stupid'. Many may well be highly intelligent, whether or not they perform poorly.

5) If difficulties are apparent, analyse the cause, then try to correct it. Try not to leave left-handers to their own devices if they appear to be having difficulties. The solution may be quite simple.

6) Never single out a left-hander in front of others if they are performing poorly, for example with handwriting. This might seem fairly obvious for any child, but some children have experienced this at school and developed psychological problems as a direct result.

7) Teachers should not assume that anxious parents of left-handers are over-reacting if they are concerned about their child's performance, particularly with handwriting. As they are closer on an individual level to their child, and may be a party to any confidences, they are more likely to have an inkling if something is wrong.

8) Parents of left-handers should keep an eye on their child's performance and analyse the source of any difficulties. It should not always be assumed that left-handedness is the cause, without good reason. There may be other factors in addition to left-handedness.

9) Communication is essential. Often, the last person to understand the nature of difficulties in school, and at home, is the child. Children may believe themselves to be less able than their peers, clumsier, or more awkward, and so on. If left-handedness is attributable to any difficulties they experience, it should be explained sympathetically and clearly, so that they understand that there is nothing to worry about and do not develop complexes.

10) Left-handedness may be present in addition to other educational difficulties, such as Developmental Dyslexia and Attention Deficit Disorder, and is thought to constitute a high percentage of special educational needs children. It is as well to recognise that some of the problems experienced by left-handers will compound these difficulties, particularly in handwriting.

Footnotes:

1   Broca, P., in S. Dimond. *The Double Brain* (London: Churchill-Livingstone, 1972).

2   Broca, P., cited in L. J. Harris, in Herron, J. (Ed.). *Neuropsychology of Left-handedness* (New York: Academic Press, 1980). Pages 3-78.

3   Jackson, J. H. in J. Taylor (Ed.). *Selected Writings of John Hughlings Jackson* (New York: Basic Books, 1958).

4   Weisenberg, T. and K. E. McBride. *Aphasia: A Clinical and Psychological Study* (New York: Commonwealth Fund, 1935).

5   Hardyck, C. and R. J. Haapanen. *School Psychology* (Vol 17, 1979). Pages 219-230.

6   Coren, S. *Left Hander* (London: John Murray, 1992).

7   Geschwind, N. and A. M. Galaburda. *Cerebral lateralisation. Biological mechanisms, associations and pathology. I. A hypothesis and a program for research* (Archives of Neurology, 42, 1985a). Pages 428-459.
    – *Cerebral lateralisation. Biological mechanisms, associations and pathology. II. A hypothesis and a program for research* (Archives of Neurology, 42, 1985b). Pages 521-552.
    – *Cerebral lateralisation. Biological mechanisms, associations and pathology. III. A hypothesis and a program for research* (Archives of Neurology, 42, 1985c). Pages 634-654.

8   Salvesen, K. A., L. J. Vatten, S. H. Eik-Nes, K. Hugdahl and L. S. Bakketeig. *Routine ultrasonography in utero and subsequent handedness and neurological development* (British Medical Journal, 1993).

9   Bakan, P. *Abstract 18* (Canadian Psychology, Vol. 28, 2a, 1987).

10 Bishop, D. *Using non-preferred hand skill to investigate pathological left-handedness in an unselected population* (Developmental Medicine and Child Neurology, 26, 1984). Pages 214-226.

11 Allele (allelomorph): *'Either of a pair of genes in the same position on both members of a pair of chromosomes and bearing characters inherited alternatively according to Mendelian law.'* (Collins Concise English Dictionary.)

12 Annett, M. *Left, Right, Hand and Brain: The Right Shift Theory* (Hillsdale: Erlbaum, 1985). Annett believes hand preference is based on hand skill.

13 McManus, K. *The inheritance of Left-handedness* (Biological Asymmetry and Handedness, Wiley, Chichester: GBA Foundation Symposium 162, 1991). Pages 251-281.

14 McManus, I. C. and M. P. Bryden. *The genetics of handedness, cerebral dominance and lateralisation* (Handbook of Neuropsychology, Vol. 6, Child Neuropsychology, Elsevier Science Publishers BV, 1992).

4 ASSOCIATED LEARNING DIFFICULTIES

There are a number of well-defined specific learning difficulties which can affect either left-handers or right-handers and for which a wide array of professional advice is now available. Parents may find their child's left-handedness is associated with a defined learning difficulty, so it is useful to be aware of the major categories of these.

Dyslexia

About 10 per cent of children are known to be dyslexic. The word comes from the Greek, meaning 'difficulty with words or language.' ('Dys' = difficulty, 'lexis' = words.) It has been given a multitude of labels (see Definitions) but is more commonly classified these days as a specific learning difficulty. It was first identified in 1896.

Dyslexics may be perfectly bright children who are quite able in some disciplines. The main feature is that their reading, writing and spelling abilities do not measure up to their intellectual ability. They may also have problems with numbers. They may understand the concept of maths but find it difficult to express on paper, or they may not understand the basic concepts of maths at all.

The cause has been attributed to an unusual arrangement, or 'wiring', of brain cells, which affects certain functions of the brain. Because of the wealth of astonishing discoveries about the brain revealed by the more sophisticated equipment we now have, scientists from the European Dana Alliance for the Brain celebrated European Brain Day in 1998 with events around the country.

Nowadays, scanners are helping scientists understand more clearly the workings of the brain. Findings have enabled new programmes to be developed to help dyslexic children improve their reading very quickly. Some dyslexics who have difficulty processing hard consonants, such as 'ba', 'da', and 'ta' are now learning to master them in experiments with the use of computer-simulated voices.

New technology even enables scientists to predict whether young babies will be dyslexic. Scientists from Yale University recently used magnetic resonance brain imaging to study the difference in reading between dyslexics and non-dyslexics. They proved that reading difficulties are linked to faulty brain circuitry, providing a physical basis for dyslexia.

With the right support and encouragement, dyslexic children can achieve in the same way as their non-dyslexic peers, performing well at university and in their chosen careers. Dyslexic achievers include Albert Einstein, Beryl Reid, Susan Hampshire, Su Pollard, the Duchess of Gloucester, Tom Cruise, Duncan Goodhew, Ruth Madoc and Michael Heseltine. (At least four of these are known to be left-handed.)

Some scientists believe that dyslexics have language spread across both hemispheres and that messages become jammed up in the Corpus Callosum. While the brain can identify an inanimate object through sight, if language is involved, confusion arises in interpreting certain letters. Around 25 per cent of dyslexics are thought to show left hand preference, not necessarily just for writing. Over 70 per cent of dyslexics lateralise late. Around 45 per cent of dyslexics are cross-laterals and it is thought that some of their difficulties are caused by writing with the left hand and sighting with the right eye, because the hand writes from left to right while the dominant eye fixes on the right side of the page. [1]

It would appear that, in dyslexics, although the left hemisphere is poorly developed impeding development of verbally-based skills, poor motor skills may have a bearing on handedness, rather than cerebral lateralisation.

Psychologist Dorothy Bishop points out the dangers of assuming that if a poor reader is left-handed, they could be diagnosed as dyslexic. *"Because people believe that left-handedness is an indicator of an unusual and a possibly disadvantageous neuro-logical organisation, a left-handed poor reader may be more likely than a right-handed poor reader to be referred to a neurologist. Further, given that there is a belief that left-handedness is part of the symptom complex of developmental dyslexia, this diagnosis may be more readily made if a poor reader is left-handed. Then a link between dyslexia and left-handedness may be forged by people's preconceptions about the significance of left-handedness.*" [2]

Dyslexia and left-handedness, however, have several things in common. More boys are affected than girls. It sometimes runs in families. Both dyslexic and left-handed children can become the classroom rebel or clown if they are labelled 'thick', 'lazy' or 'stupid', as sometimes happens. They can develop behavioural problems through frustration if their difficulties are not recognised and provided for.

A number of the difficulties attributed to both are similar, although they may display other difficulties which are not common ones. Common symptoms include:

a) Fastening buttons, shoelaces, ties.
b) Left-right confusion, poor sense of direction.
c) Undetermined hand preference.
d) Poor handwriting.
e) Reversals:
    i) numbers, for example: '15' for '51', or '2' for '5'.
    ii) letters, such as: 'b' for 'd', and 'q' for 'p'.
    iii) words, for example: 'saw' for 'was'.
f) Mirror writing – writing from right to left of page in reversed letters.
g) Poor short-term memory:
    i) forgetting signs and symbols (including numbers, formulae, graphs and charts) creating difficulties in maths (arithmetic).
    ii) confusing words to nursery rhymes.
    iii) forgetting arithmetic tables.
    iv) forgetting instructions.
    v) inability to remember names or put names to faces.

h) Clumsiness, disorganisation.

i) Using fingers or making marks on paper to calculate.

j) Confusion over places, times, dates.

k) Inattentiveness, lack of concentration.

There may be other signs, but if a child displays several of the above difficulties, they may be dyslexic. From this, it can therefore be seen that a left-hander who may be perfectly able at some activities, but bad at reading, writing and spelling, and who has several of the above difficulties, may be rightly or wrongly labelled dyslexic.

One of the most common queries received by the CLHS from anxious parents is whether or not their left-handed child is dyslexic, because their writing is poor and they are being harassed at school for being 'lazy' or 'not trying hard enough'.

A classic example of this was the eight-year-old Manchester boy who was becoming emotionally disturbed because of the constant criticism of his poor handwriting at school. The problem was finally solved when his mother spotted some scribble in his workbook telling her that he was trying hard but couldn't see what he was writing. Because he wrote with his left hand, he was pushing his arm towards his body, and covering his work. The boy, who was very bright, was not dyslexic but he did have other difficulties and needed assessing. Unfortunately, as is often the case, the waiting list was so long that he would have been in secondary school by the time the assessment was available.

Dyscalculia

About 60 per cent of dyslexics have difficulties in arithmetic, particularly in speed and fluency of simple calculations, although they may have good mathematical ability. Some cannot represent calculations on paper even though they are able to carry them out. They are often labelled 'lazy'. Others cannot calculate at all and have no understanding of the basic concepts. About 11 per cent excel and 29 per cent are no different from children without learning difficulties.

Favourite (P...) Animal

My Animal is a Radit
Igiv it is Sum water
Tev it sum foowd And
I put it in the (cat) cal
and we get sum water
evriy day and we got sum
fwood for the rabit
and (ws) we gid it sus foow

The handwriting of a left-handed girl showing dyslexic spelling tendencies.
(From *Laterality Report*, Centre for Left-Handed Studies, 1992.)

Difficulties encountered include: slowness in simple calculations, memorising multiplication tables, counting up and counting backwards, remembering to carry figures, directional difficulties, subtraction, multiplication, division, copying down correctly, rules and formulae memory. Poor short-term memory and inability to grasp abstract concepts may be contributory factors.

Attention Deficit Disorder

Attention Deficit Disorder (ADD) and Attention Deficit Hyperactive Disorder (ADHD) often co-exist with dyslexia. Its causes are not known, although it is thought to be hereditary and the possible result of a chemical imbalance or a shortage of neuro-transmitters in the brain.

The term Minimal Brain Dysfunction was applied in the 1960s but recently the term was changed owing to parents' misconception that their children were brain damaged.

ADD children display poor attention span and are easily distracted, leading to daydreaming and switching off. They may be restless and fidgety, its more extreme form being hyperactivity. They tend to be impetuous or impulsive, acting without thinking, and are poor planners. They fit in the category of clumsy child and have poor co-ordination for fine motor tasks, such as tying shoelaces and legible handwriting. Gross motor difficulties include hopping, skipping, kicking and catching balls.

Short-term memory is poor, particularly for the spoken word. Many children are over-assertive or aggressive and inflexible, with temperamental mood changes. Some experience sleeping problems and many either eat constantly or have eating disorders. Speech disorders can occur, sometimes a stutter, developing into difficulties with reading and writing.

Not all ADD children will have all symptoms. Those who have co-ordination difficulties are usually cross-laterals whose laterality has not formed. This can resolve when the part of the brain affected matures. [3]

Left-handedness, cross-laterality and undetermined-handedness, it must be noted, are not the cause of learning difficulties or other disabilities as has been stated (more mythology). However, they may occur in addition to them.

GUIDELINES **2**

1) Special teaching in the school two or three times a week should be tried first, separate from the mainstream, until the child's abilities have improved sufficiently for them to join their class again. If this does not help, consultations should be held with parents, the school doctor and an educational psychologist to find the cause and determine appropriate action. As this may be a long-winded process, parents may wish for an additional assessment outside school. They should apply to their family doctor, or local dyslexia association, for details of specialists in this field. Others who might help include an occupational therapist; or physiotherapist where movement control is linked with poor handwriting; or an orthoptist for visual problems.

2) Parents must be kept informed of the child's progress at all times and schools must be told of any outside assessments or specialist education parents may be contemplating. Head teachers can send certification of difficulties from an educational

psychologist to examining boards, if examinations are being undertaken, providing that the child has been assessed.

3) Recognise that the child has a problem. Don't urge a child to try harder or admonish him for being 'lazy'. Discuss any difficulties and explain what the problems are. Be supportive and uncritical.

4) A child may not wish to learn at home after a day in the school-room, so parents are advised not to force them to do this, unless the child is happy to do so. Then check with the teacher to make sure you are not using conflicting methods.

5) Don't make comparisons to the child with more able classmates or siblings.

6) If there is a reading problem, don't compel the child to read out loud in front of others. Try reading out loud to the child yourself. Suggest looking at words in detail, a few letters at a time. A bookmark can be helpful so the words can be read line by line. Pupils with left : right confusion may find the 'look and say' method counterproductive. If a teacher or parent sits with a child and reads out loud from left to right, the child may be following from right to left, thereby learning the wrong words. Although it seems to be discouraged somewhat nowadays, finger pointing by the reader is probably the best means of counteracting this tendency.

7) If there is a spelling problem, writing words out repeatedly in an effort to memorise won't make any difference.

8) If there is a handwriting problem, don't chastise if written work is untidy or illegible. Copying and re-writing will not help. Cursive handwriting is probably the best style to adopt, because of its natural flow from left to right which should prevent directional problems. Because the letters are joined to one another, it should cut out the tendency to reverse letters. (See Chapter 7, page 61.)

Writing on alternate lines is a good idea so that the teacher can read the writing more easily. Make corrections near to the errors instead of at the end of the exercise. If there are a lot of mistakes, writing comments rather than making rows of crosses, will be less demoralising. Coloured highlighters are also less off-putting than red pens. Remember that writing may be hard work for the child. For an older child, a typewriter may be very helpful, or a word processor with a spellchecker.

9) Copying instructions from a blackboard can result in errors if there is a hand : eye co-ordination problem. Write them out for the pupil and read out the instructions, making sure they are understood. Parents should reinforce this by reading them out as well. A tape recorder can help sometimes for remembering instructions.

10) Highlight the activities the child undertakes well. Praise the child to help build self-confidence and, above all, give the child encouragement.

Footnotes:

1   Hornsby, Dr. B. *Overcoming Dyslexia* (London: Vermilion Books, 1997).

2   Bishop, D. V. M. *Handedness and Developmental Disorder* (London: Erlbaum, 1990). Page 87.

3   Serfontein, Dr. G. *The Hidden Handicap* (Australia: Simon and Schuster, 1996).

5 SCHOOL PROJECTS

The South Paw Club

In July 1991 a unique club was launched during hymn practice at a London High School after an enterprising teacher noted the difficulties left-handed pupils were experiencing when writing.

Gwen Dornan, who teaches handwriting at Lytton House, the junior department of Putney High School, had an overall view of all the left-handers in the school, aged between 5 and 11. As each individual could only easily share her experiences with one or two class members, it seemed feasible to launch a group where the older girls could help the younger ones. *"Difficulties could be discussed and perhaps the little ones would understand why I was trying to persuade them to write with their hands below the writing line when they saw the 11-year-olds using fountain pens,"* explained Gwen Dornan.

She was encouraged by other members of staff, including the only left-handed teacher. When it was realised that the final year left-handers were quite a successful group, it was decided to go ahead and launch the South Paw Club [*]. Each prospective member received an invitation stamped with a left paw print and on joining, was given a club badge. About 10 per cent of the school now belong to the club, which meets every three months. One meeting a year has been set aside for handwriting, but other issues are tackled during the other sessions.

At the first meeting, the older girls demonstrated their handwriting skills, writing below the line with the paper at the correct angle. All the girls attempted writing with their right hands and mirror writing. The second meeting consisted of a discussion on the advantages and disadvantages of left-handedness.

An exercise for the girls to seek out famous left-handers, resulted in a fine display of pictures, which involved parents contacting libraries, friends and organisations for help. Other sessions involved tests of dominant feet and eyes and an enquiry into the incidence of left-handedness in the pupils' families.

The overall result has meant that the younger children's handwriting has improved considerably and they have responded well to the older children's advice. The Club has been so successful that right-handers are wondering why they, too, cannot have their own club.

Glasgow Prize Competition Winners

At another school, in Glasgow, nine curious schoolboys, eight of them right-handers, carried out a fact-finding task on left-handedness which earned them Glasgow Prize Competition certificates for work of outstanding merit.

The boys, from Kelvinside Academy, thought up their research idea because they were intrigued by the three 1992 Presidential candidates who were all left-handed. They thought that if Bill Clinton, George Bush and Ross Perot were all south paws, perhaps left-handers were high achievers.

Supervised by their maths teacher, the nine asked all pupils to fill in questionnaires. When the answers were computed, they found that left-handers did not make better tennis players, as has been suggested, and that they are not more academic. But they did find that left-handers were either very good – or very poor – at art.

[*]The term 'South Paw' is now given to left-handed boxers, although it originated as a baseball term, from the Chicago West Side stadium where left-handed batters faced south. 'Rocky' was a south paw boxer and, as such, only considered useful as a sparring partner.

South Paw bear and his team of
Little Bearers are left-pawed.
(Picture courtesy of The Left-Handed Company, Manchester.)

GUIDELINES 3

1) Why not launch a South Paw Club in your school, based on Putney High School's example?

2) Carry out an investigation into left-handedness, as a project, which could also involve right-handed pupils. Parents could join in with the research, too.

6 LEFT-HANDER FRIENDLY EQUIPMENT

According to the CLHS survey, 63 per cent of teachers were aware of the left-handers in their classes, without checking. 79 per cent of the total sample said they made adjustments to help. Of these, 46 per cent provided left-handed scissors and 28 per cent made sure they placed the left-handers on the left of desks. Very little else was being done.

Only 17 per cent of parents provided left-handed scissors, 23 per cent thought they were already provided by the school and 11 per cent thought that schools should provide them. At home, 43 per cent of left-handers had difficulty using normal potato peelers, 26 per cent could not master knitting or sewing skills, 23 per cent were confused by cutlery and 17 per cent could not cut with right-handed scissors. Tying shoelaces, using knives and pens and confusion between left and right sides also presented difficulties.

Why should these tasks present so much confusion to left-handers? What can be done to help?

Left-handed Utensils

Nowadays, there are several outlets where left-handed equipment can be bought to make life easier for left-handers, young and old. In the U.S.A., almost every State boasts a left-handed store. In France, left-handed scissors can be bought at most supermarkets. In Germany, they are supplied in schools. In Britain, left-handed items can only be bought at specialist shops and mail order outlets. Some educational catalogues include scissors, as do a few hardware shops and department stores, although more often than not, they are not reverse engineered.

Utensils, such as knives, with cutting edges on both sides of the blade, can now be bought widely. Yet some left-handers like to use an exclusively left-handed item and, sadly, shoppers often find themselves the butt of derision from unenlightened shopkeepers when asking for them.

Prices for left-handed items are higher than for the right-handed equivalent. This is not because suppliers are taking advantage of the left-handed, as is often suggested by the cynical, but for the following reasons:

a) Manufacturers must reverse their machinery or tool up specially, which is expensive.

b) Staff who are used to making items for right-handers work more slowly on left-handed items.

c) The market is small, so it is not considered cost-effective to make goods for a minority.

Below are outlined some educational items which left-handers find difficult to use if they are not specially designed for them. Often, the left-handed versions are thought of as gimmicks by people who are not aware of their true usefulness and importance.

Equipment List

Pencil Grips

These are brightly-coloured rubber or plastic grips which are moulded to the shape of the thumb and index finger. They fit neatly

on to a pencil or ballpoint pen and can be turned one way for right-handers and the other for left-handers. More comfortable and compact than the longer versions, they help to correct the grip, preventing the tight clutch which left-handers often tend to make. It ensures that the fingers are held at the correct point on the writing implement.

Sloping Boards

The slope of the boards (20 degrees) ensure that left-handers cannot fall into the bad habit of making an inverted hand posture, or hook, above the paper. The writer is forced to sit upright with eyes about 30 cm from the paper. Slouching is prevented and the pencil lines up with the hand and arm, co-ordinating the writing action. It prevents tight gripping of the implement which occurs on a flat surface. They can be bought in plastic with a recess for writing utensils or in hardboard with a plastic fabric surface and are equally suitable for right-handers. As the surface may be hard, pupils should always write on a pad or book to create a resilient surface, and never use a single sheet of paper against the board. [1, 2 and 3.]

Sloping boards are simple and cheap to make. One 6' x 4' sheet of hardboard will make 19 boards. For the cross strut and legs, use 1¹/₂" x 1" PAR. Pad the board with five layers of flat newspaper and a sheet of sugar paper and fix with Sellotape. The surface must be completely flat. [4]

This left-handed girl had cerebral palsy. The sloping board supports her arm and helps minimise tremor, but it would be of benefit to any writer. Pads or books should be used on the board, not single sheets of paper as some resilience is needed.
(Original from R. Sassoon, 1995.)

Cartridge Pens

Pen nibs are pushed towards the body and tend to stick in the paper, making a hole. If pressure makes the nib cross over, the ink does not flow. When a child, in frustration, shakes the pen, ink blots result on the paper which are then smeared by the hand. When I was at school, you could always tell a left-handed child by the inky shirt cuffs. Left-handed oblique nibs curve slightly to the left and move smoothly across the paper.

Calligraphy

Calligraphy and italic pens with nibs designed for left-handers are available. In addition to single dip nib and cartridge pens, there are basic, master and de luxe calligraphy sets containing a variety of easy change nib units. Recommended are a Platignum fountain pen with an Italic B2 Left Oblique nib. This may be bought separately or as part of an Italic set which includes a fountain pen and five nibs. With the Osmiroid fountain pen, Pelikan 4001 ink is suggested to help the flow. The nib should be a left-hand medium 30 degree oblique model. A good dip pen is the Higgins Speedball C-0 Left and C-2 left nib and pen nib holder, for large letters, headlines and titles. With the correct equipment and guidance, left-handers make good writers and calligraphers.

Rulers

Left-handers draw lines from right to left which means that, with a conventional ruler, they are covering up the numbers. If they need to keep removing their hands to see the numbers, they are in danger of moving the ruler while drawing. A left-handed ruler has the zero on the right and the numbers running towards the left.

Scissors

Scissors come in sizes from 4" to 6" for children and larger for adults. Left-handled scissors, with the handles merely reversed for comfort, are not left-handed. Right-handed scissors, sold as ambidextrous are right-handed scissors with two sharp blades which may be dangerous for a child. Scissors for young children should have round-ended blades for safety. As the blades on both these types of scissor are not reverse engineered, the child cannot see the cutting line. Left-handed scissors have the blades reversed and biased together. The blades of right-handed scissors are biased apart so that if a left-hander uses them, the material slips against them without cutting. The cutting line is obscured because the blades are on the wrong side. Left-handers who have acquired a right-handed bias by using conventional scissors will find it difficult to change to left-handed ones. Some will cut with their right hands, others use right-handed scissors in their left hands and turn them upside down. It is better to introduce young left-handers to their special scissors from the start.

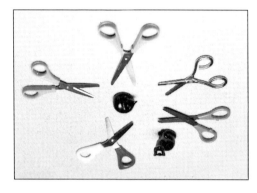

A selection of children's left-handed scissors with reverse engineered and round-ended blades for safety.

(Picture courtesy of author.)

Compasses

Many left-handed children find it difficult to use compasses. Often, they exert too much pressure, as they tend to do with writing implements. Some have orientation difficulties. School compasses are frequently loose and move with little manipulation from the child. Some plastic covered compasses obscure the view of the point. A larger than average compass is recommended, the sort used for posters or flip charts. The Rahmqvist Universal Compass has an arm which locks the compass into position and it also takes a thick implement. Producing large circles with this enables the child to get used to the feel of using the instrument. From there, a spring-bow compass from an educational supplier is the next step. These are similar in size to school compasses. The integral lead is harder to break when pressure is put on it than a normal lead pencil. Teachers should guide the movement with their hand over the pupils' to help them get the feel of the instrument. [5]

Desks

Nothing can be more uncomfortable for a left-hander than trying to take notes during a lecture or conference in a chair which has a right-handed rest, as many do. Work stations can be obtained which can swing to the left or the right. (See Suppliers, page 113.)

Keyboards

Left-handers are at an advantage with the normal QWERTY keyboard because 57 per cent of typing is done with the left hand. The problem occurs with numerics, which are always on the right. Attempts to produce an alternative keyboard biased to the right were made in the 1940s. Its lack of success was attributed to the fact that people tend to resist change. Millions of people would have had to relearn their existing skills and millions of keyboards would have had to be changed.

There are companies that sell special keyboards. Maltron, the ergonomic keyboard specialists, sell two-handed keyboards which have proved beneficial for people with dyslexia. They also supply single-handed keyboards and mouth/headstick keyboards for special needs. (See Suppliers, page 113.)

The Keyboard Company in Stroud supplies a special left-handed keyboard with the numeric keypad section on the left hand side. The KBC 3500 is identical to a standard keyboard in all other respects.

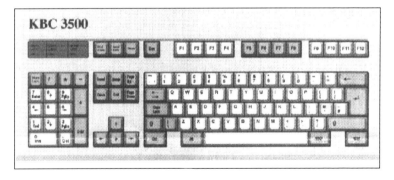

The KBC 3500 – Left-handed Keyboard.
(Picture courtesy of The Keyboard Company.)

The same company also supplies an ergonomic Colani designed left-handed mouse in light grey or black adapted to the shape of the left hand. It works with IBM AT/PS1/PS2 and compatibles and Apple Macintosh Classic/SE/II/Quadra and other computers. (See Suppliers, page 113.)

Household

For the older child and adult, peelers, paring knives, cook's knives, can openers, breadknives, corkscrews, pastry forks and a host of other kitchen implements are on the market, with cutting edges on the right-hand side.

Conventional implements with cutting edges on the left do not work well in left hands because the food will be cut at the opposite angle.

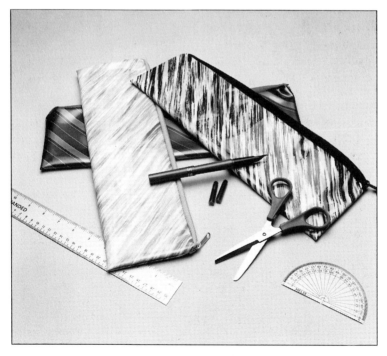

The Left-hander's School Survival Kit for children comprises scissors, pen and ruler in a zip-up case.
(Picture courtesy of author.)

GUIDELINES **4**

1) Make sure the left-hander is placed on the left of a double desk or at the left-hand side of any table both in the classroom and at the lunch table. Clashes of elbows with right-handers can result in fist fights. They should never have a wall on their left.

2) If there are a few left-handers in the class, try to seat them together to avoid elbow clashes, but avoid segregating them altogether from the other children or you may be in danger of making them outcasts for no good reason.

3) Ensure that left-handers can see the blackboard without twisting.

4) Make sure they have enough room as they will be working at a different angle to the right-handers and may take up more space.

5) Help them with tools and equipment, particularly those designed for right-handers. Make sure they are not likely to have any accidents by stretching across for controls, by becoming entangled in flexes or cutting themselves on sharp implements.

6) Explain practical instructions carefully. Remember, logic and short-term memory may not be among the strong points of some left-handers and they may not assimilate information as quickly as right-handers. You may have to demonstrate visually before they will retain information.

7) Demonstrate some tasks, such as handicrafts, by facing left-handers so they see a mirror image of themselves (except when writing, or this can induce mirror writing). They can then copy your actions without twisting and contorting themselves and displaying any right/left confusion.

8) Try carrying out some actions with your left hand, including writing. This may help you to appreciate some of the difficulties they experience with right-handed implements.

9) Ensure that left-handed utensils are available, particularly scissors, and that they do not get locked away in a drawer and forgotten or mixed up with the right-handed scissors. This can be avoided by putting the left-handed ones in wallets or by ensuring they have handles which are a different colour

from the right-handed scissors. Some baby scissors (4") have the word 'Lefty' inscribed on them; others have one yellow and one green handle for easy identification.

Children may be too embarrassed to tell you they are struggling if their peers are managing well or they may not realise their problem is a left-handed one. Investigate your best sources of supply. If schools or parents can get together some bulk orders, they may be able to negotiate a discount for quantity.

10) If you know of someone who is studying the subject for a thesis or dissertation, or if you are aware of a local person who is an authority on left-handedness, invite them into school to talk either to the children or to the teachers about the subject – they will find it quite fascinating and it may be an ideal sounding-board for sharing ideas. There is no reason why any parent or teacher could not read up on the subject and deliver their own talk. (The author of this book gives illustrated talks to schools, colleges, INSET days and dyslexia meetings.)

Footnotes:

1   Brown, B. and S. Henderson. *A Sloping Desk? Should the Wheel Turn Full Circle?* (Handwriting Review, 1989).

2   Myers, P. Wallis. *How the Sloping Board Assists Pencil Hold and Writing Action in Young Children* (Handwriting Review).

3   Charlton, C. and G. Kavanagh. *An Improved Sloping Desk Top: a Controlled Trial in South Australia Schools* (Handwriting Review, 1994).

4   Myers, P. Wallis. *Handwriting in English Education* (Visible Language, Vol. XVII, No 4).

5   Lowy, S. A. *And with your compass, draw a circle...* (Handwriting Review, 1991). Pages 83-84.

7 LEFT-HANDERS AND HANDWRITING

Many children suffer from difficulties in producing clear and legible handwriting. It is not a problem confined to the left-handed. Some education authorities pursue a policy of emergent handwriting, letting pupils develop their skill unaided, while some schools introduce one of the many commercial schemes on the market, depending on what their budget will allow, which means the best scheme is not always chosen.

In a 1982 survey, 12 per cent of 10-year-olds in a London borough had serious handwriting difficulties. [1] In the International Literacy Year (1990), around four million adults in the U.K. were experiencing reading and writing difficulties, 40 per cent of them in relation to writing only.

These difficulties, if uncorrected, do not go away. They simply follow the child into adulthood, with severe ramifications. They show up on job application forms and are reflected in any written work necessitated in the workplace, deteriorating further as the need for speed dictates.

Children who write with their left hands may experience problems of a different kind, in addition to those experienced by their right-handed peers. It should be noted that not all left-handed writers experience these difficulties but, even so, a great deal depends on the training they receive from their teachers. It is no use labelling a child's handwriting 'illegible' and 'messy' if the child has experienced no guidance or tuition in the first place.

Reluctance to write may well result and/or the development of behavioural problems through frustration. The child tries hard, makes no headway and gives up. He becomes the classroom 'clown' and is admonished for being 'lazy' and not 'making an effort'.

Handwriting Difficulties

What are some of these handwriting difficulties?

a) Orientation: writing from right to left of the page in reversed letters (mirror writing).

b) Reversing letters, numerals and symbols.

c) The writer cannot see what is written as the writing hand is angled over the writing.

d) Untidy work, smudging, due to the hand pushing towards the body across wet ink or streaking of ballpoint ink.

e) If using ink pens, nibs may stick in the paper whilst the hand pushes across the body, making a hole. The ink does not flow freely causing the writer to shake the pen frequently and create blotches on the paper.

f) Slowness in writing, particularly at junior level, although left-handers usually catch up by secondary level. Slowness is due to digital manipulation, the fingers and thumb doing all the work without any wrist action. The hand and arm have to be moved from time to time to see what has been written, which may also slow down the writing.

g) Angling the paper in the wrong way, so that the writing hand obscures the work.

h) Poor grip – the writing implement is usually gripped very tightly, too close to the tip for control, obscuring the view of written work. This also creates muscle fatigue in the fingers.

i) Inverted hand posture: the hand curls around the top edge of the paper, forming a hook. Then the writer can see under the hand but this tends to 'over the top' writing with the wrist humped on top.

j) Poor posture, particularly leaning over to the left or bending low over the paper.

What can be done to help them? In general, right-handers have formed their writing habits by the age of 11, but left-handers, on the whole, have not, so they can still be helped. Some left-handers, however, are very dextrous and learn to write well, long before this.

Paper Position

Left-handers, when writing, develop a variety of techniques. Mainly, they either write with the hand below the writing line or they advance from the left side of the paper and make a 'hook' with the wrist above the paper (inverted hand posture). The first group slant the paper clockwise and the second slant it anti-clockwise, similar to the right-handed writer.

Many different variations of these two positions can occur. Six have been noted for the former and nine for the latter. [2] Some children, however, prefer the paper horizontal, to the left or right of them.

It is generally considered that the first technique is by far the best for left-handed writers to use and that they should write in this way. However, more advanced pupils, who have already formed the habit of inverting their hand when writing, may find they are unable to change their technique.

In this case, only one of the nine variations has been recommended, even though it is not ideal, and an adjustment to this variation could be encouraged.

The paper is turned to the left, as if for a right-hander.
The wrist is turned on the edge enough to allow maximum flexing.
(Original from E. A. Enstrom, 1962.)

Mirror Writing and Reversals

Much conflicting research has been published on this topic over the decades. Reasons given have included mental deficiency, heredity, eye, hand and brain abnormalities, developmental eccentricity, neurosis and defective vision. It was first noted in medical research in 1698 in an epileptic girl. It has also been found as the result of hypnosis, inebriation, trance, hysteria and changeover of handedness. [3]

Writing and reading from right to left of the page and reversing characters from left to right or upside down when writing are common traits among non-right-handed children. It should be mentioned that right-handed children also do this and it usually clears up unaided.

Using a pointer on a blackboard or whiteboard and a finger when reading from a book, writing drills and word tracing have all been suggested in the past as aids. However, correct diagnosis of the difficulty followed by the appropriate treatment is recommended nowadays, in the light of the availability of more advanced knowledge.

If mirror reading, or writing, continues after six years of age, it can signify that the child has dyslexia or dyspraxia (an inability to plan, organise and co-ordinate movements, often 'clumsy' children with handwriting difficulties). It can also be due to an instability of eye movement and/or difficulties of binocular eye convergence.

When reading, writing and spelling, the right and left eye should converge at a distance of around 30 centimetres for near vision, so that a single picture of the print is received. A normal eye examination may not identify this problem because the eye charts used are not appropriate for the way in which a child carries out close work.

If faulty eye convergence is suspected, the child should see an optometrist, who recognises diseases and abnormalities and can recommend eye exercises. [4]

If the child becomes tired and complains of headaches, screws up or rubs the eyes frequently, it may indicate convergence difficulties. Strange spelling with reversals can be the result of poor visual recall and eye problems. Tracking exercises are recommended for correcting left to right eye movements. [5]

Expert Advice

A number of eminent consultants have studied left-handed writers in depth and written about their difficulties and how they can be overcome. With their help, we can at last present the sort of accurate guidelines that parents and teachers are constantly asking for.

Caution should be exercised in asking for advice of this type from people who do not have the relevant qualifications, expertise and knowledge, likewise from printed material which has not come from an expert source. For example, manufacturers and suppliers of left-handed goods have not necessarily studied the vast literature sufficiently in depth to be able to advise, nor are they likely to be experts in handwriting skills.

Some advice has been repeated by more than one consultant, albeit expressed in different ways, but these points have been left in if only to emphasise the need for their implementation.

On certain issues, there are two schools of thought. One viewpoint is for those left-handers who have already formed poor writing habits or who need to follow their natural tendencies as left-handers, to be provided with models recommended to help them. The opposite viewpoint is that they should follow right-handed models and work in the way accepted by the majority, for example, backward vs forward sloping writing; right vs left stroke direction when forming letters; inverted vs vertical hand posture.

Each left-hander should try the various suggestions and advice given and adopt whichever will work best for them to produce legible and speedy handwriting.

GUIDELINES 5

AUDREY McALLEN –
MOVEMENT EXERCISES TO ASSIST LEFT-HANDERS

(Audrey McAllen has extensive experience as a Class Teacher in Waldorf schools, and has developed both diagnostic and remedial exercises now taught in training centres in the U.K., Australia, Europe and North America. She is author of *'Teaching Children Handwriting'*.)

We are born into a right-handed world where practicalities are orientated for the convenience of right-handed people. This is fine for the baby, toddler and young child, who live in total empathy with this world. The child bonds with the mother, follows her around, copies everything she does and extends this innate faculty of imitation throughout his surroundings. This is how children attain their skills and the mastery of their bodies.

But some bodies won't obey the laws. A hand is held out to receive an apple. The voice says, *"No, not that hand – use the other..."*. The apple is thrust into the hand *not* extended and promptly dropped. For the muscles of the right hand were not prepared to receive it as were those of the hand held out. So begins the steady growth of blocks and tensions in the child's spontaneous movement.

How can we loosen these blocks and tensions when, after appropriate tests, it is decided that this child is truly left-handed? How can we help him to feel comfortable in his body and enjoy the effects of natural rather than thwarted movement? The following exercises are especially helpful in developing handwriting skills and comfort for left-handers. The exercises involve first large body movements, then the more delicate movements needed in handwriting.

The Whirl

One of the first dynamic scribbles of the child is a whirl, which children usually enjoy drawing while kneeling on the floor. Kneeling allows full movement of all arm and shoulder muscles.

So let our left-hander recapitulate this by kneeling, with a large piece of paper on the floor in front of him, using a fat stick crayon in the left hand to build up a whirl-pool, bird's-nest or ball of wool, whatever picture is suitable for his age. Accompany the child in this activity with your own drawing. First, slowly, then quickly, then with eyes shut. Have races to see who can cover the paper first. (Even teenagers enjoy this activity as their thwarted natural movements are released!)

Pendulum and Cross

The next drawing of the scribbling stage is the pendulum – swinging movements, from one side of the paper to the other. Don't dictate the side on which to begin – the child's body will make its own adjustments.

Emulate the scribbling phase of the toddler again by adding up and down movements to the pendulum to create a cross. This drawing reflects the structure of our body, which appears, as a result of the unique human capacity to stand upright in space, at around one year old.

After enjoying these activities on the floor, transfer them to a table and repeat them, using appropriate, comfortably sized paper.

Loops and Lines

Now move on to patterns: loops, straight lines in rhythmic sequences, three loops to two straight lines... Preferably, paint these first, with a flat paint brush, then draw them with the crayon. The forms should be over 6 inches (15cm) high, using arm and shoulder, as well as hand, movement.

Left-Right Balance

This next movement activity helps develop a conscious feel for the relationship between the left and right of the body. Parents, teachers – experience this yourself, first!

Place both hands, palms down, in your lap. Raise them up at the same time. As they come level with the head, divide them with the natural outward circular movement for the right and left sides of the body, returning them to your lap. This is the basic movement for each side of the upper half of the body – clockwise on the right, anti-clockwise on the left.

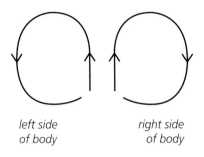

left side of body   *right side of body*

Now stand up. Take one step forward, and then another. Observe the natural swing movement of your right and left hips as you walk. It is opposite to your arms. The right hip and foot swing slightly toward your body – anti-clockwise. The left hip and foot swing slightly clockwise as you walk. The above and below movements of the body balance each other. This can be demonstrated diagrammatically, as in the palindrome alongside.

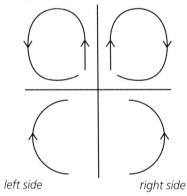

left side   *right side*

This mirroring shows the basic vertical line of the body, the midline division between the left and right side of the body and the horizontal midline division of above and below and represents the cross of our skeleton, the vertical cross of left-right, above-below.

Eye-Hand Co-ordination

Alphabetical letter forms also appear in children's scribbles at some point. Early scribblings and drawings lay the foundation for the skills needed for writing and literacy, that is eye-hand co-ordination. If there are undue interruptions to normal development, or premature demands on the child for too early formal learning, these movement systems can become jangled together and the resulting problems given labels such as dyslexia, dyscalculia, dyspraxia or non-right-handedness. If the individual is left-handed anyway, this does not make acquiring the necessary skills any easier.

The whirl, pendulum and pattern exercises can be done from six years of age. We should also accustom the child to saying the alphabet forward and backward, accompanying each letter with a ball-throwing exercise, or by stepping as he says each letter name. Such exercises, and those that follow, allow the wonderful self-corrective structural system of nerves, muscles and bones to help sort out such tangles. The ages for the following exercises are as stated.

Ball Twirling Exercise (From eight years.)

Place three tennis size balls on the table. Ask the child to pick up one (observe which hand). Holding the ball in the cup of the hand facing towards him, show him how to reach with his thumb over the ball towards the little finger and begin to twirl the ball round and round. Take another ball in the other hand and repeat this. Then, with both hands in movement, stand up and lift the hands in a graceful curve.

Now add foot movements. Place a ball in front of the feet and tell the child to put his foot lightly on it and roll the ball inwards round and round, controlling the ball with the sole of the foot. Build up the movements: first use just one hand, then add the other hand, and finally add a foot. When all is in movement, speak a rhyme. Repeat the exercise using the other foot.

The practice of large spontaneous body movement should help the child release tension and through the acquisition of new skill, rebuild lost confidence.

Fine Motor Skills (From six years.)

These exercises with smaller movements help the fine motor skills.

Marble Rolling

Pick up a marble with the fingers of the left hand and circle it around on a piece of paper in front of you. Its natural movement tends to follow the arm movement – anti-clockwise. Let it wander across the page and back.

Now repeat using a clockwise movement. Not so easy! So practise revolving the marble between the thumb and first and second fingers turning it away from the body and then towards the body. Count aloud – the numbers spoken as the movement is taken over by the thumb. When this becomes easy – then say the alphabet. Both forwards and backwards!

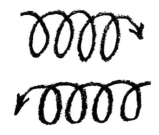

With the marble resting on the paper and held between the fingers as if it were a pencil, form a circle, anticlockwise and clockwise. Now move across the paper and back, using the clockwise movement left to right, and the anticlockwise movement on return. Start this on both sides of the paper, but after a period of practice, always start on the left. Now try straight lines.

Another important movement sequence to practise is the spiral, both anticlockwise and clockwise. This is the basic movement of the lower case letters, and synthesises the left/right, up/down, and in/out (corresponding to forward/back) movement of the early scribbles of the child. Let the child draw and walk this form in a variety of ways.

Spinning a top from a child's game also helps to make the fingers skilful.

The Counting Star (For left-handed children from age six.)

Here is an exercise which will consolidate all we have done: it helps to eliminate any residual mid-line problem and addresses hand-eye and speech co-ordination. The variety of movement changes, while keeping the handwriting direction constant, helps the child to feel comfortable and secure in himself.

The exercise is done using a fat wax crayon and facing a blackboard or a large sheet of paper, at least 26" x 24" (66 cm x 60 cm), according to the pupil's height. The feet should be slightly apart, but kept parallel during the exercise. To make sure that the child does not change his central position in front of the circle, and so avoids crossing the mid-line, get him to draw round each foot and stand in this form. It is important that the pupil does not slouch or have the body weight more on one leg than the other.

Make a circle with 12 equally spaced points. Start at point 12 and count on five points. Draw a line from the starting point to the fifth point. From there, count another five points. Draw from the end of the first line to the new position. The arm should be fully extended and the drawing made with large sweeping movements making the whole body active in expansion and contraction. Repeat, going in a clockwise direction, until the line returns to the starting point.

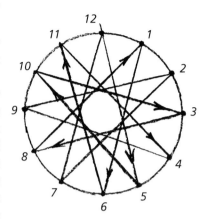

The clockwise direction of writing is maintained, even when the pupil is left-handed. When given as homework, the star may be coloured in. Any number of points in a circle may be chosen. The lines must intersect, touch each point and return to the starting place. The arm must be extended to its full length when drawing from one point to the next, so that a sweeping movement is used.

See that the left hand moves with the counting – which should be spoken aloud. The right hand should mark the position to which the line is to be drawn. Always move clockwise.

Below are the number sequences for the circles which, when counted, go to each point and close the circle producing a star. For example, on a circle of 12 points counting with either 5 or 7 will go to each point and make a star.

Number of Points	Counting Numbers
5	2
7	3 or 4
11	4, 5, 6 or 7
12	5 or 7
13	5, 6, 7 or 8
15	4, 7, 8 or 11
17	4, 7, 8, 9, 10 or 13
18	5, 7, 11 or 13
19	5, 6, 7, 8, 10, 11, 12, 13 or 14
20	7, 9, 11 or 13

Writing the Roman Letters

It may well be an advantage to recapitulate the drawing of the capital letters, which can be found in any calligraphy manual, to see that the strokes are in the correct sequences. (Incidentally, I find that children tend to respond better to parents or teachers using the term *'correct'* rather than *'right'*.)

The Roman Capitals are composed of straight and curved strokes. The straight strokes reflect the directions of space implicit in the vertical and diagonal crosses, the left/right, up/down of the vertical, and the diagonals which give the perspective of forward/backward. By working with capital letters we can establish comfortable pencil hold, and the sitting and paper positions described in the previous sections of this book.

Cursive Writing

Finally, we come to cursive writing. First, simply say the letter "O". As the lips form the sound, let the child feel them with the fingers and notice how they form into a circle. Ask him to look into the teacher's eye and observe the circle of colour, with the little black dot which can change size but always remains a perfect circle.

The circle is the form in which the body of all the clockwise and anti-clockwise movements of the cursive letters can be made. We only need to put their ascender and descender strokes at the appropriate side. The 'm', 'w' and 'x' require two circles – and we can even introduce the old form of 'z'. (Children love to be challenged by something special.)

Taking the form "O" as our model allows the child, in due course, to imprint his own personality and style into his writing as fluency is acquired.

Cursive Writing Practice

Start by writing the longest word in the world – the alphabet. In doing this we practise all the variations of entry and exit strokes and if we speak the letter and the direction in which our pencil moves we

abcdefghiyklmnopqrstuvwxyz

zyxuvuritsrqpomnlkjihgfedcba

shall be integrating eye, hand, and speech, a very useful acquisition for reading.

Keep the paper well to the left of the body, as the wobbles may start when crossing the midline during the development of fluency.

Now return backwards:

Initially, these letters need to be written quite large (letter body height about 1cm) so that the hand movements are made conscious as the directions are spoken. When the correct directionality has been established, a natural height can evolve.

abc cde efg: abcde fghiy

zyxuvuv vritsr rqpomn

Practise the letters in consecutive groups – saying the alphabet forward and back as we have practised in stepping on each letter as we walked forward and back, in ball throwing, for example. Then the consciousness in letter forming is not disrupted by having to think how to spell.

Hopefully, regular practice with the various exercises will help left-handed children to produce, with fluency and beauty, their own personalised handwriting.

References:

Gaddes, William H. *Learning Disabilities and Brain Functions* (New York: Springer Verlag, 1985). Pages 226-228, 246.

Kellogg, R. *Analysing Children's Art* (Mountain View: Mayfield, 1970). Pages 66-67, 250, 262-3.

Salter, Joan. *The Incarnating Child* (Stroud: Hawthorn Press, 1987).

Strauss, Michaela. *Understanding Children's Drawing* (London: RS Press, 1996).

DR. ROSEMARY SASSOON

(Dr. Rosemary Sassoon is an eminent writer and lecturer on handwriting tuition. She has written several noteworthy books, including *'Handwriting: The Way to Teach it'* and *'Handwriting: A New Perspective'*. The University of Reading awarded her a Ph.D. for her work on the effects of models and teaching methods on children's handwriting. Her advice to teachers is specifically aimed at ensuring that left-handers' needs are met.) [3]

1) Place the paper to the left side and slant it to suit the writer, rather than allowing the child to adapt the body to suit the paper position. This way, the line of vision will not be interrupted and it will deter them from making a 'hook' or inverted hand posture and from being forced to lean the body over sideways. Check that there is sufficient space on the table for them to be able to do this and that the left-handers sit on the left side of their right-handed friends, so there is no clashing of elbows.

   Corners made from coloured tape could be pasted on the desk of those children who find it hard to remember the most comfortable paper position, or they could use a paper overlay with the position marked on it.

2) A pencil with a soft lead is best for left-handers as it will not dig into the paper. Non-smudge free-flowing modern pens, such as fibre tips, are best.

3) Ensure the seat is sufficiently high for the pupil to see over the hand.

4) The lighting should be checked to ensure that the left-handers are not writing in the shadow of their own hands. This can happen if the classroom is laid out for the convenience of right-handers, particularly if desks are in rows, and the light comes from the side suitable for right-handers.

5) The penhold should be far back enough from the tip for the pupil to see what they are writing. The index finger can be as near to the point as necessary – it is the thumb that obstructs the view and this should be held further back. Different penholds

will be required for different types of pen, particularly felt tips, which need to be held in a more upright position. An alternative method is to hold the pen between the index and the middle fingers.

6) Exercise books generally have printed material for copying on the left and a blank page on the right. This creates an obstruction for the left-hander whose left arm will be covering the work to be copied. The ideal would be to have special books for left-handers, with the layout reversed.

7) Left-handers find it hard to slant their letters forwards, so they use a backwards slope. A special handwriting model with a slight backwards slope would be a good idea.

backward sloping

A backward-sloping model might encourage left-handers whose writing slants backwards.
(Reprinted from R. Sassoon, 1995.)

8) Left-handers find it hard to follow demonstrations by right-handers. The best way to deal with this is for teachers to demonstrate with their left hand, on an individual basis, no matter how shaky the handwriting may look. It will also help right-handed teachers to understand the difficulties faced by left-handers.

9) Left-handers automatically draw lines from right to left so when learning to write, some of them may find it hard to remember to begin on the left of the page and they may begin instead on the right, writing backwards in mirror writing.

Use a visual reminder of the starting point, such as a red vertical strip of paper or plastic clipped to the left of the page, or something more novel, to get the child's own imagination working to help overcome the problem. (See diagrams on the following pages.)

Some pre-writing exercises are also helpful.

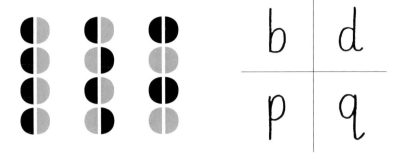

Any material can be used for matching, pairing and making patterns with semicircles to help develop mirror-image discrimination (left). This is another method to highlight letters that are almost mirror images (right).
(Reprinted from R. Sassoon, 1995.)

10) Reversed letters may also occur. To help combat reversals, try linking 'a' to 'd', suggesting the pattern 'adadad', using 'add' or 'dad' as a reminder; 'b' and 'p' make the pattern 'bpbpbp', with 'pub' as a reminder.

11) It is easier for a left-hander to form some letters, such as 'o', and the circular part of 'a', 'd', 'g' and 'q', in a clockwise direction, and they tend to begin where the letter should finish. This right to left movement often goes unnoticed and unchecked. This tendency means that they will experience some difficulty when it comes to joining up letters.

One of the obvious signs that this is happening is uneven or extra-wide spacing between letters, but often it can only be detected by watching the child actually write. It will be hard to correct once the child has formed the habit. It should be looked for and corrected at an early stage. They may also find the letters 's' and 'f' difficult at first and will reveal this by making them larger.

12) Poor spacing between words may indicate incorrect paper position or the need for an eye test.

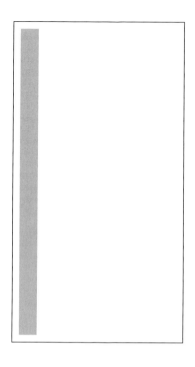

This tinted strip on the left of the paper reminds the left-hander to begin writing on that side.

The clown strip was supplied by 9-year-old Sophie Lovett and the pen portrait by a younger child. The teacher should say "start on the side with the tall boy (or clown), and always start at the head."

(Reprinted from R. Sassoon, 1995.)

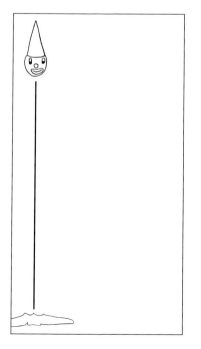

PRUE WALLIS MYERS

(Prue Wallis Myers is a former H.M. Inspector for Art and General Education. A handwriting tutor, she also lectures and writes on the subject and has made a particular study of difficulties encountered by left-handed children.)

Three Different Ways of Manipulating the Pen for the Left-hander

The inverted position or the humped up wrist position is not included. In each of these ways, the paper should be turned down 30 degrees on the right with the right edge opposite the centre of the body.

1) Using Digital Manipulation

Here, the action of making a downstroke is by pulling the pen back into the hand through fingers and thumb and then releasing it out again to make the diagonal upstroke (see Diagram 1). In this position, the pen lines up with the forearm, which is away from the body and makes an angle of 45 degrees to the table edge.

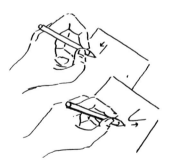

Diagram 1: Pulling the pen into the hand to make the downstroke and thrusting it out again to make the diagonal upstroke.

2) Using Wrist with Fingers and Thumb

Here the hand is turned slightly outwards on the wrist. The action is by pivoting the hand on the wrist, as well as pulling the pencil into the hand with fingers and thumb. The wrist swivels forwards to line up with the forearm in making the upward stroke. The fingers and thumb are also released forwards at the same time. The forearm is only a little way out from the body in this position (see Diagram 2).

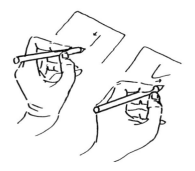

Diagram 2: The hand is turned slightly outwards on the wrist, which pivots slightly round to the right in making the upstroke.

3) Using Finger Swinging Manipulation

Here the pen is held high in the hand, in front of the knuckles, close to the second joint of the first finger. The hand is positioned knuckles uppermost. Action is by swinging the first finger back and forth on its hinge joint (see Diagram 3). In this position the pen may be unstable in the hand, as it is not locked through the tripod grip (finger and thumb coming into contact with each other and the pencil and the second finger holding underneath).

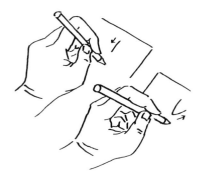

Diagram 3: Here the pen lies well in front of the knuckle related to the movement of the first finger hinge joint as it swings back and forth.

DR. JEAN ALSTON

(A freelance chartered psychologist, author and lecturer, Dr. Jean Alston has for many years worked with teachers on undergraduate and in-service courses. She lectures to teachers and therapists throughout the U.K., and is the author of several books, including *'Writing Left-Handed'*, an advice booklet for parents and teachers of left-handed children. Her ten major rules for left-handed writers, detailed below, help to sum up her recommendations.)

As with right-handed pupils, posture and paper position are the factors which influence all others.

1) Select a writing surface and chair suitable for your own height. Ideally, the seat should slope slightly forwards, and the writing surface should slope slightly down towards the body. Sloping desks were frequently used in earlier classrooms and offices. Left-handers sometimes find it helpful to have a higher than usual chair, so that they can see their writing more easily.

2) Sit towards the right of the desk or table, leaving plenty of space for writing on the left side of your midline. This will allow plenty of space for the elbow to move backwards and forwards, and prevent the left arm from becoming too constricted, close to your body. If you sit beside a right-handed writer, make sure that he or she sits by your right side.

3) The majority of the paper should be to the left of your body midline, also helping you to avoid bringing the writing arm too close to the body.

4) Tilt the paper up to 32 degrees in a clockwise direction. Pen movements can then be towards and away from the body, and the writing is likely to be slightly forward sloping as with right-handers.

5) Left-handers sometimes push the pen or pencil point into the paper as they write. Make sure that you have a pencil point or nib which does not do this. You need a smooth pointed nib or a soft B leaded pencil.

6) Many pens have metallic or slippery barrels. These are not helpful for left-handed (or right-handed) writers, but they may encourage left-handers to hold them particularly tightly and also to press heavily on the paper surface.

7) Always support the paper with your right hand. Left-handers are inclined to push the pen or pencil, so holding the paper steady is particularly important.

8) The barrel of the pen or pencil should point towards the left shoulder. It should be below the writing line, allowing you to see the words you write.

9) Keep your writing forearm parallel with the paper edge as you write. Trials with the paper edge and the forearm parallel to each other, but at varying degrees, will help you to find the best position for you.

10) Hold the pen or pencil up to two centimetres from the point, so that you can see the words as you write them. Look for a pen with rubber, soft or moulded plastic where the fingers should hold, or one which prevents your fingers from sliding towards the nib or point.

Research has shown that left-handers who develop an inverted hand posture (hooked grip) usually steady the paper by placing the right hand below the line of writing and towards the left of the page. The hands then cross as the writer writes, creating further difficulty for seeing what is written. To avoid this and the later inverted hand posture, the steadying hand should be placed towards the paper's right edge.

Many pupils are told to keep the writing paper 'squarely' or 'straight' in front of them, which causes many problems. The ten guidelines should help the pupil to find their own most comfortable position and should help to develop comfortable writing and a fluent individualised style.

This alphabet can be adapted for separate letters of cursive handwriting and fits the hand movement. Ideal for left and right-handers. The simplest style for the hand to make.
(Lettering by Prue Wallis Myers.)

Left-handed Teachers

While much is made of left-handed children and their difficulties, little help is given to left-handed teachers faced with a roomful of right-handed pupils who may well be confused by instructions and demonstrations conducted the wrong way round for them. Beryl Cowen, a left-handed teacher from Cheshire, would change classes and teach science instead of teaching needlework to right-handers.

She tended to begin in the wrong place when she demonstrated, so used rhymes and word games to help her. For example, when writing an 'i' she would say: *"Start in the middle, straight down and put his hat on."* For an 'n', she wrote from right to left, so said to herself: *"Start at the left, and up and over the bridge and down. I have to remind myself of the correct direction first. I can't do it on the board."*

She also found cursive handwriting difficult to teach. *"Some of the curves and letters go the wrong way,"* she maintained. *"I find the 'z' difficult to write."* She did not recommend the Marion Richardson method for left-handers. *"If the writing is neat, tidy and readable, I don't think one form should be favoured over the other. The Marion Richardson slopes in the wrong direction for a left-hander."*

Writing with the Non-preferred Hand

Some right-handed children who have suffered an accident or who have a weakness in their preferred hand, may have to change to the left hand. This could have an adverse effect on their sequencing of letter joins and they will need individual guidance on this and the new paper position and writing implement. [6]

Left-handers are far more adept with right hands than right-handers are with their left hands, because they have had to adapt to a right-handed world. This is actually one of the greatest advantages of being left-handed. In fact, many left-handers have no problems at all and write perfectly well.

The main point of this exercise can be summed up best by Rosemary Sassoon when she states: *"All these aspects need to be woven into a policy that spreads awareness of left-handers' needs and ensures that they are met"*. [7]

There is no reason why schools should not have a policy for left-handers, rather than either overlooking them or wondering how on earth to help them.

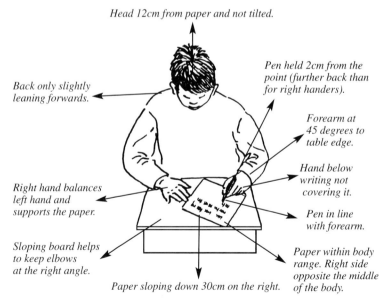

Head 12cm from paper and not tilted.

Pen held 2cm from the point (further back than for right handers).

Back only slightly leaning forwards.

Forearm at 45 degrees to table edge.

Hand below writing not covering it.

Right hand balances left hand and supports the paper.

Pen in line with forearm.

Sloping board helps to keep elbows at the right angle.

Paper sloping down 30cm on the right.

Paper within body range. Right side opposite the middle of the body.

A good position for the left-handed writer.
(Illustration from Prue Wallis Myers.)

Footnotes:

1   Rubin, N. and S. E. Henderson. *Two Sides of the Same Coin: Variations in Teaching Methods and Failure to Learn to Write* (Special Education: Forward Trends, Vol. 9, No. 4, 1982). Pages 17-24.

2   Enstrom, E. A. *The Relative Efficiency of the Various Approaches to Writing with the Left Hand* (The Journal of Educational Research, Vol. 55, No. 10, 1962). Pages 573-577.

3   Paul, D. *Living Left-Handed* (London: Bloomsbury, 1997).

4   Alston, J. *Writing Left-Handed* (Manchester: Dextral Books, 1996).

5   Pollock, J. and E. Waller. *Day-to-Day Dyslexia in the Classroom* (London: Routledge, 1997).

6   Sassoon, R. *Handwriting: The Way to Teach it* (Cheltenham: Leopard Learning, 1985). Page 19.

7   Sassoon, R. *Handwriting Problems: A different view of the written trace.* Paper presented at the Association Typographique Internationale, 6th Working Seminar, Hamburg, 1989. Reprinted in Handwriting Review, 1985. Pages 64-69.

8 LEFT-HANDERS AND CRAFTS

Crafts such as pottery or sculpture should pose few special problems for the left-hander as these types of activity require the ability to use both hands. However, some handicrafts can cause considerable difficulty to the left-hander because the only instructions available have been written for right-handers.

A frequent plea from parents of left-handers is: *"How do I teach my child to knit?"* Knitting pattern publishers overlook the needs of left-handers who cannot follow their patterns and I have found no books on handicrafts which give instructions for people who work in reverse. Trying to follow normal instructions facing a mirror involves considerable contortion, and the book has to be picked up and put down while all this is going on – not very satisfactory at all.

There are four possibilities.

1) If you are right-handed, become the mirror image yourself. Sit the pupil opposite you so that they mirror all your actions. This way their left hand will be doing what your right hand is doing.

2) Stand behind the pupil and guide their hands. This means that they will have to work right-handed, but depending on how mixed-handed they are, they may well be able to work the right-handed way. I was taught to knit this way by a right-hander.

3) Use any instruction book and read left for right. I learned to crochet this way, but only mastered basic stitches. The more complicated the instructions, the more confusing for a left-hander.

4) The final option is for the pupil to follow the instructions below to learn the basic steps, and work left-handed, but to date I know of no knitting patterns designed for left-handers so right-handed patterns will have to be followed in reverse.

Space does not allow for instructions other than those that cause directional difficulties. Any knitting book will contain advice on the rudiments of knitting, equipment and tension. We give first the Continental method of knitting, which is quicker than our own, followed by a potted version of the traditional method. The pupil can then choose whichever way suits best.

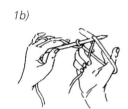

1a)

GUIDELINES 6

Knitting the Continental Way

1) Casting On

a) Make a slip knot, leaving about two feet of yarn hanging, and with your left hand, put a needle through the loop. The hanging piece should be held in the right hand and the wool you are going to work with should be held in your left hand, wound between your fingers.

1b)

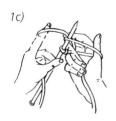

b) The right hand yarn is then looped round the needle from behind, going above the needle and pulling tightly.

1c)

c) Make a loop with the wool in your left hand, wind it up and around to you from behind the needle, so it is on top of the first loop.

1d)

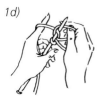

d) Pull the top loop through the one behind it which then comes off the needle.

e) Pull both ends of the wool to
    tighten (not too tight) and you have
    your first stitch.

1e)

f) Carry on making as many loops as
    you need around the needle.

2) Knitting in Garter Stitch

a) Hold the second needle in your left
    hand and the needle containing
    your stitches in your right hand.
    Wind the wool through your left
    fingers as before so that the wool
    runs through gently as you work.
    The wool you are working with
    should hang behind the needles.

2a)

b) Push about one inch of the left
    needle into the first stitch on your
    right needle, wind the wool from
    your left hand behind the tip of the
    left needle and round to the front
    and pull it through the stitch on the
    right needle with your left needle
    and let this new loop move on to
    the left needle.

2b)

c) Pull the wool gently to secure it.

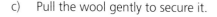

d) Continue along the row of cast on
    stitches until you have knitted a
    whole row of new stitches. If you
    want to work in garter stitch only,
    the empty needle is always held in
    the left hand when starting each
    row. Every stitch and every row is
    knitted, creating a raised surface.

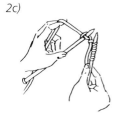
2c)

3) Working in Purl

a) The wool you are working with should hang in front of your needles. Push about two inches of the left needle under the top of the first stitch on your right needle, loop the wool round both needles (up and round the left needle from left to right) and pull the loop through the first stitch on the right needle with the end of the left needle.

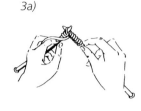

3a)

b) Place the new stitch on your left needle and drop the old stitch off the right needle.

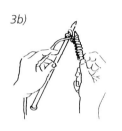

3b)

c) Carry on making loops in this way so you have a whole row of purl stitches and change over needles to make a new purl row.

4) Knitting in Stockinette (Stocking) Stitch

3c)

a) Make one row of knit stitches and one row of purl stitches, continuing in this way throughout your work.

5) Ribbing

a) Knit in combinations of knit and purl stitches on the same row. For example, knit 1, purl 1, knit 2, purl 2, etc., depending on the pattern you wish to produce.

b) Make sure you have enough stitches cast on to take an even division of the knit and purl combination you choose.

c) When you turn your work to begin a new row, always begin with a knit stitch if you ended on purl and vice versa.

6) Increasing

a) To increase stitches, knit into your first stitch and, without removing it from your needle, put your left needle into the back of it and knit the loop in addition to the stitch.

b) Move both stitches from the left on to the right needle so you have an extra stitch.

7) Decreasing

a) To decrease stitches, put your left needle at the bottom of two stitches and knit them together, pulling both off your right needle on to the new loop. This gets rid of one stitch.

8) Casting Off

a) When you have finished your work, knit two stitches on your left needle, put the tip of your right needle under the first stitch you knitted and pull it over the second stitch, so that it drops on to your work below neatly.

8a)

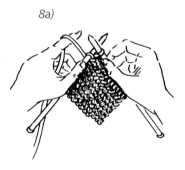

b) Knit another stitch and repeat the procedure, then another until all the stitches have been cast off, except the last.

8b)

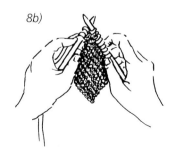

c) Widen the stitch and remove your left needle. Pull the wool through the loop and cut it. Then finish off with a knot.

Knitting the Traditional Way

1) Casting On

a) Place two fingers of your left hand between the wool and the ball and make a slip knot on one needle.

b) Place the second needle upwards through the loop, pass the wool between the two needles and bring the point of the left-hand needle through the loop on the right-hand needle. This makes a second loop, which is then placed on the right-hand needle.

c) Repeat these directions until you have the number of stitches you require. Keep each stitch fairly loose so that it slips up and down the needle easily. If four needles are in use, for example for a sock, continue casting on to three needles, which will make a triangle when beginning the first round.

d) The cast on edge should be firm or it will stretch when the garment is worn, so in the next row, knit into the back of each stitch to ensure firmness.

2) Plain Knitting

a) Hold the needle containing the cast on stitches in the right hand and place the left-hand needle through the first loop upwards. Pass the wool, from the back of the work, over the point of the left-hand needle. Make a loop, as for casting on, and slip the first loop off the right-hand needle.

b) Continue doing this to the end of the row. On beginning the next row, slip the first stitch from one needle to the other without knitting it, as this makes a neater edge. Continue to slip the first stitch of each row.

3) Purling

a) Hold the cast-on stitches in the right hand, bring the wool forward to the front of the work, put the left-hand needle through the front of the first loop with the needle pointing downwards.

b) Pass the wool round the point of the left-hand needle. Draw it through the loop to make a new stitch and drop the old one off the needle.

c) Continue doing this to the end of the row.

4) Increasing

This should be done at the beginning or the end of a row. Knit into the back and the front of a stitch, making an extra one. If you need to increase a large number of stitches, do so at the beginning of a row by casting on.

5) Decreasing

Knit two stitches together. If you need to decrease a large number of stitches, knit two stitches, slip the first over the second and let the second one drop off.

6) Casting Off

Work with the wrong side of the work facing. Knit the two first stitches. Slip the first stitch over the second with the right-hand needle and let it drop. Continue until one loop remains. Break off the wool, leaving five or six inches. Slip it through the loop, pull tightly and darn the end into the work with a sewing needle.

Abbreviations

When following knitting patterns, the abbreviations are as follows:

k.	= knit plain.
p.	= purl.
tog.	= together.
wl. frd.	= wool forward.
st.	= stitch.

Learning to Crochet

Practice with a large hook, using wool, rather than cotton, to begin with. Make a loose ball of wall, to avoid straining the yarn.

1) Chain

a) You need a chain to begin. Hold the end of the wool between the thumb and second finger of your right hand. Pass the strand round the first finger, from the side nearest to you.

b) Bring the wool round to the right of the circle this makes, hold the loop in place with your thumb and pass the strand over the middle and under the third finger, then over the fourth.

c) Hold the crochet hook as if writing, slip it under the loop where it crosses the top of your finger and draw the wool through.

d) Slip the loop off your first finger and draw the wool up to the hook. You now have your first stitch.

e) Hold the end of the stitch between your thumb and forefinger, near to the hook. Pass the wool from the ball over the first and middle fingers, then under the third and over the fourth.

f) Pass the hook under this strand from right to left, hook the wool and draw it through your first stitch. Repeat this until you have the length of chain needed.

g) Be careful not to pull the stitches too tight, checking your tension so that it fits the pattern you are following.

h) While making the chain, move your right hand along it every three or four stitches, so that it is held close to the hook.

2) Single Crochet (Slip Stitch)

Work a length of chain. Put the hook through the chain next but one to the hook. You should then have two loops. Pass the hook under the wool from right to left and draw it through both loops. Continue to the end of the row. When you turn, make one chain. Put your hook through the next stitch to that and draw the wool through both loops. At the end, turn again, with one chain. To help keep the surface even, put your hook through both the loops of the previous edge (or through one) when working in rows.

3) Double Crochet

Work a length of chain. Pass the hook through the third stitch from the hook, then under the wool from right to left and draw it through. Now you have two loops. Pass the hook under the wool and draw it through both loops. Repeat in each stitch. At the end, turn with two chain. For the next row, put the hook into the next stitch, draw the wool through, pass the needle under the wool again and draw through both loops. Repeat this. Always turn with two chain.

With these basic stitches, you should be able to learn the other stitches needed for crochet, for example half-treble, treble, double treble, triple treble, picots, squares, blocks and scallop edging. Any instruction book can be followed by reversing the directions, reading left for right and vice versa. Learning to chain and work the basic stitches with the left hand is the biggest problem.

Abbreviations
When following crochet patterns, the abbreviations are as follows:

CH.	= chain.
d.c.	= double crochet.
tr.	= treble.
d.tr.	= double treble.
t.tr.	= triple treble.
s.c.	= single crochet.
sl.	= slip.
sp.	= space.
rep.	= repeat.

9 LEFT-HANDERS AND MUSIC

There is no reason why left-handers should not enjoy making music just as much as right-handers. Most musical instruments – such as woodwind, brass or percussion – should present few problems to left-handers, but stringed instruments may do so if the left-hander wishes to play the left-handed way. Not all left-handers will have this problem, but choice of sides depends on orientation preferences, as with guitar playing.

String players in an orchestra sit together and if one of them bows in the opposite direction, it not only looks untidy but they might be in danger of poking their neighbour's eye out. A viola player in the City of Birmingham Symphony Orchestra had to use her left hand after an accident and was placed slightly apart from the others. Charlie Chaplin played the violin left-handed in the film *Limelight*, with the strings reversed.

Left-handed violins are not made. These would have the sound holes facing the wrong way which means that instrumentalists would be playing to opposite sides of the hall or to the back wall. The violin is designed to be held in the left, not the right, hand and the higher notes would be less accessible if played the wrong way round.

Probably the best instrument to learn would be the French horn, which is valved for left-handers.

The piano demands dexterity by both hands and while suitable for left- or right-handers, the bass may well dominate when played by a left-hander. Concert pianist, Christopher Seed, felt that only a reversed keyboard would do the left-handed pianist justice and recently commissioned the world's first left-handed piano with the treble keys on the left, the bass keys on the right and reversed pedals. Limited demand and high costs would probably make mass production prohibitive.

The American composer Ned Rorem, wrote Piano Concerto No. 4 (for Left Hand) for pianist Gary Graffman who had a malady in two fingers of his right hand. André Previn conducted its world premiére at the Philadelphia Academy of Music, followed by Carnegie Hall, New York in 1993. It was not the first piece for left hand, however. Previous works were composed by Ravel, Prokofiev, Britten, Richard Strauss, Franz Schmidt and Paul Wittgenstein. (The Disabled Living Foundation has masses of music written for the left hand.)

In music lessons, left-handers who prefer to conduct with the left hand may do so in reverse. It may prove impossible to persuade them to conduct with the right hand because of their confusion over stroke direction. The other thing to watch out for is in music theory, when they may write the ticks on their quavers, semiquavers and demi-semiquavers back to front.

One of the most popular instruments is the guitar. We are often asked for left-handed guitar chords or for details of left-handed guitars.

Left-handed guitars are rather more expensive than right-handed guitars, because of the time and expertise needed to make them. More information is available from suppliers listed on page 114.

Left-handed guitar
built by Fender.
(Picture courtesy of
Arbiter Group PLC.)

The chords can be worked out in reverse. A few of the more often used ones are illustrated here. Some advice on stringing the guitar for the left hand is also given. This is not a lesson on how to play the guitar and such information, together with details of the different parts of the guitar and principles of music, can be gained from any guitar tutor book or through private tuition.

GUIDELINES **7** Playing the Guitar

1)   Stringing the Guitar

If you don't have a left-handed guitar, you will have to change round the strings on a conventional one for left-handed play. The lst and 6th strings (E treble and E bass) will be changed over. The 2nd string (B) will be swopped with the 5th string (A) and the 3rd string (G) will be swopped with the 4th string (D).

Attach the strings to the bridge. Remove the pin, make a knot at the end of the string, put it into the hole and replace the pin. If there are no bridge pins, push the string through the hole from the soundhole side, bring the end forwards and put it under the string behind the saddle. Pass it behind the bridge with the end between the back and the string.

Pass the other end of the string over the roller and through the hole from underneath. It then goes over and under itself. When the machine is turned, the end of the string can be gripped between itself and the roller.

Strings 1 and 6 are secured to the rollers nearest to the nut. Strings 3 and 4 are secured to the rollers farthest from the nut. Strings 2 and 5 go to the centre pair of rollers on each side.

2)   Holding the Guitar

Sit on a chair with your right foot on a low stool and the waist of the guitar on your right thigh. The fingerboard should be at an oblique angle. The head should be held at the height of your right shoulder, about a foot in front of the horizontal shoulder line. The position can be adjusted for personal comfort.

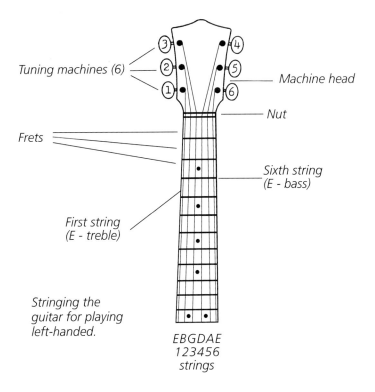

Tuning machines (6)

Machine head

Nut

Frets

Sixth string
(E - bass)

First string
(E - treble)

Stringing the
guitar for playing
left-handed.

EBGDAE
123456
strings

3) Left Hand Position

Rest your left arm on the top edge of the instrument so that your left hand falls over the string near the soundhole. The strings should deflect almost parallel to the table when struck by the thumb and the tip of the fingers. Hold the wrist in line with the arm.

4) Right Hand Position

Do not hold the neck in the hollow between thumb and forefinger. The thumb should be halfway under the neck. The right hand fingers should be just behind the frets. When strings 1, 2 and 3 (treble) are stopped with the right hand fingers, the thumb should be halfway under the neck. When strings 4, 5 and 6 (bass) are played, the right wrist should be moved outwards so the thumb moves towards the treble part of the neck. The elbow should be as near as possible to the waist of the instrument and the right palm should never hit the neck. The hand should be moved as little as possible when fingering.

5) Tuning

If a piano, pitch pipe or tuning fork is available, tune the lst string to the E above middle C. The others are B, G, D, A and E continuing down the scale. To tune by ear, pluck string 1 (E). With third finger of right hand on 5th fret of string 2, pluck with your left thumb. This should make the same sound as the E string, when plucked. Pluck string 3 with 2nd finger on 4th fret. This corresponds to the 2nd string open (that is, not held down). Pluck string 4 with 3rd finger on 5th fret. This sounds like string 3 open. Pluck string 5 with 3rd finger on 5th fret. This sounds like string 4 open. Finally, pluck string 6 with 3rd finger on 5th fret. This sounds like string 5 open.

6) Guitar Chords for Left-handers

The letter 'o' which appears on the chord diagrams means that this is an open string which is not played. Touch the string marked with the fleshy part of one of the right hand fingers to mute it when struck.

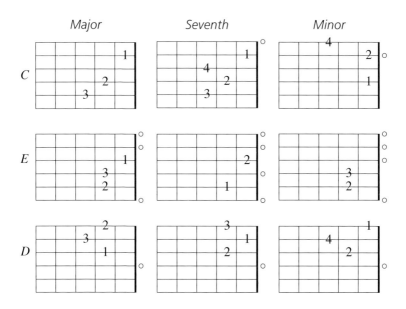

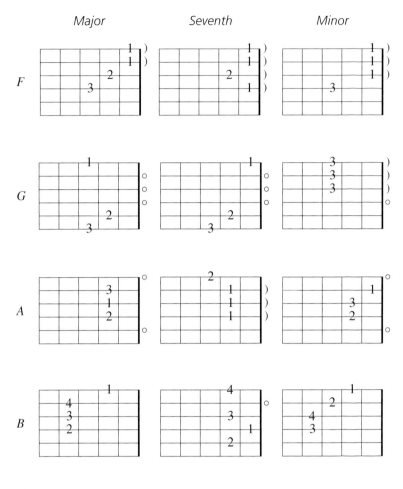

	Major	Seventh	Minor

7) Notation

The notes are marked on the chords in numbers. These denote the fingers which must be placed on the frets. The corresponding fingers of the right hand are:

> 1 = index finger
> 2 = middle finger
> 3 = ring finger
> 4 = little finger

A slur over two or more notes means that they are all played by one finger.

10 GUIDE FOR STUDENTS

Students undertaking GCSE or class projects or theses on left-handedness are often left-handed themselves or have a left-handed child and they would like to know more about the subject.

They begin, believing it will not be a difficult task, but find, quite early on, that they are unable to locate any relevant research material. Libraries, for some unknown reason, do not appear to keep any. At university level it is easier. Even so, material is limited. Often, students will want to know how to undertake some experimental testing. Some suggestions are outlined below.

Laterality Testing

People are not just left- or right-handed, nor are left-handers simply mirror images of right-handers; we have established elsewhere that there are various degrees of handedness. Apart from choice of direction of handedness, degree differs in individuals which can cause confusion in evaluating left-handedness in a person. (See Chapter 1, Definitions, page 11.)

Although several tests exist to establish a person's laterality, they are not always indicative of true left- or right-handedness and results may vary. This can give different verdicts either after several trials of one test or after trials of several types of test. Questionnaires need to be administered about three times to be effective, and really only serve to indicate consistency of preference among various activities, not the actual strength of preference.

In general, researchers agree there are three parameters by which left-handedness may be measured:

1) Is it the hand used for writing?

2) Is it the hand preferred for certain key tasks, used consistently?

3) Is it the most proficient or most able hand?

Point 1 can be easily observed, although it may not be too obvious until the child is old enough to learn how to write properly.

Point 2 can be evaluated from questionnaires, such as the two given here. From this, a laterality quotient is found. Researchers, such as Dorothy Bishop, question the validity of preference inventories, *"...laterality quotients from such instruments fail to tell us anything about the stability of hand preference, or about the absolute or relative skill of the two hands."* [1]

When applying questionnaires, researchers must ensure that the subject carries out the tasks before answering, as actions have been found to differ from peoples' verbal perceptions of how they carry out tasks. Because several types of handedness have been noted, the first questionnaire deals only with activities involving skill, as other types of handedness have been found to be inconsistent. These include reaching actions, where either hand could be used, power actions, as in carrying heavy objects where hands may be switched, and bimanual actions, such as swinging a golf club.

Questionnaires and Tests

Handedness Questionnaire

Decide which hand you use for each activity below and tick the column that describes you best. If uncertain, act out the action.

		Left	*Right*	*Either*
1)	With which hand do you normally write?	☐	☐	☐
2)	With which hand do you draw?	☐	☐	☐
3)	Which hand would you use to throw a ball to hit a target?	☐	☐	☐
4)	In which hand do you use your racquet for tennis, squash?	☐	☐	☐

		Left	Right	Either
5)	With which hand do you use your toothbrush?	☐	☐	☐
6)	Which hand holds a knife when you are cutting things?	☐	☐	☐
7)	Which hand holds the hammer when you are driving a nail?	☐	☐	☐
8)	In which hand would you hold a match to strike it?	☐	☐	☐
9)	In which hand would you use an eraser on paper?	☐	☐	☐
10)	Which hand removes the top card when you are dealing from a deck?	☐	☐	☐
11)	Which hand holds the thread when you are threading a needle?	☐	☐	☐
12)	In which hand would you hold a fly swatter?	☐	☐	☐
	Totals:	☐	☐	☐

Count the number of 'left', 'right' and 'either' responses. Multiply the number of 'rights' by three, multiply the number of 'eithers' by two, then add both totals to the number of 'lefts'. With this total, the following table should tell your direction and degree of handedness. Around 72 per cent of people tested should be strongly right-handed and about 5 per cent strongly left-handed. Professor Coren uses similar questionnaires to measure footedness, eyedness and earedness. *(Source: Coren.)* [2]

33 - 36	strongly right-handed.
29 - 32	moderately right-handed (mixed right-handed).
25 - 28	weakly right-handed (mixed right-handed).
24	ambidextrous.
20 - 23	weakly left-handed (mixed left-handed).
16 - 19	moderately left-handed (mixed left-handed).
12 - 15	strongly left-handed.

The Edinburgh Handedness Inventory

Surname

Given Names

Date of Birth   Sex

Please indicate your preferences in the use of hands in the following activities by putting '+' in the appropriate column. If you are really indifferent about which hand to use in any particular case, put '+' in both columns.

Some of the activities require both hands. In these cases the part of the task, or the object for which the hand preference is wanted, is indicated in brackets.

Please try to answer all the questions and only leave a blank if you have no experience at all of the object or task.

		Left	*Right*
1)	Writing	☐	☐
2)	Drawing	☐	☐
3)	Throwing	☐	☐
4)	Scissors	☐	☐
5)	Toothbrush	☐	☐
6)	Knife (without fork)	☐	☐
7)	Spoon	☐	☐
8)	Broom (upper hand)	☐	☐
9)	Striking (match)	☐	☐
10)	Opening box (lid)	☐	☐

(Source: Adapted from Oldfield.) [3]

A Laterality Quotient (LQ) is obtained by scoring –100 for complete left-handedness through to +100 for complete right-handedness. The LQ is found by subtracting the number of actions performed with the left hand from the number performed by the right hand, and dividing this total by the number of actions assessed (10 in this case). Multiply the result by 100.

Hand Preference Tests

Hand preference tests are uni-manual and may consist of such symmetrically-presented tasks as throwing a ball, threading a cotton reel, hammering, using a spoon. These tests are repeated three times during a half hour interval. Responses are scored as Right (R), Left (L) or Bimanual / mixed (B). A Laterality Index (LI) [4] is calculated across all the tasks as follows:

$$LI = 100 \times [n(R)-n(L)] / [n(R)+n(L)+n(B)]$$

Handedness Test

The objects are presented with both hands along the centre. Little speech is used. Each test is repeated three times, not necessarily in the same order each time. The object is to note the inconsistency of hand choice on each item. Abnormality is present where, in children aged from five years upwards, handedness changes on three or more tasks from trial to trial.

1)   Eating with a spoon.

2)   Drinking from a cup at least one quarter full of water.

3)   Brushing the teeth with a toothbrush.

4)   Drawing with a crayon on a piece of paper.

5)   Throwing a ball.

6)   Hammering the table with a plastic hammer.

7)   Picking up a sweet.

8)   Picking up a coin.

(Source: Taken from Soper.) [5]

Hand Proficiency Tests

Point 3 can be discovered by carrying out manipulative tests, such as peg moving, used successfully by Marian Annett [6], who found that it was, in fact, the strong right-handers who could be disadvantaged. [7]

This may be slightly harder to execute as it involves individual testing, whereas questionnaires can be taken away and filled in at leisure or carried out in groups.

Ten wooden pegs in a row are moved at speed from one set of holes at the back to another set at the front. The child stands at the pegboard which is placed on a table and steadied by the examiner's hand. The pegs are moved, one by one, from right to left with the right hand and left to right with the left hand. The time is measured to the nearest 10th of a second with a stopwatch. This is carried out five times with each hand. The norm is the mean of the five trials (or three for younger children). Pegboards can be made, with holes 1.3cm in diameter, 2.2cm deep and 2.5cm apart. The pegs are made of 1.0cm dowelling, 5.1cm in length.

Footedness, Earedness and Eyedness Questionnaires

Other tests are often tried to determine the dominant feet, ears and eyes. As both hand and foot actions are motor functions, they can be linked to laterality, but the sensory functions of eyes and ears are not and should be looked at separately. Foot dominance is often determined by the first foot to begin mounting a staircase or by the consistent kicking foot. Sighting dominance tests usually consist of identifying the eye used to look through a keyhole, telescope or microscope. Research shows that 70 per cent of the population have right eye dominance regardless of their handedness. [8]

Coren's test for footedness, eyedness and earedness are similar to his test for handedness, as are the scoring methods, but the interpretations are different and are given at the end.

Footedness Questionnaire

	Left	Right	Either
1) With which foot would you kick a ball to hit a target?	☐	☐	☐
2) If you wanted to pick up a pebble with your toes, which foot would you use?	☐	☐	☐
3) Which foot would you use to step on a bug?	☐	☐	☐
4) If you have to step up on to a chair, which foot would you place on the chair first?	☐	☐	☐
Totals:	☐	☐	☐

Earedness Questionnaire

	Left	Right	Either
1) If you wanted to listen to a conversation going on behind a closed door, which ear would you place against the door?	☐	☐	☐
2) Into which ear would you place the earphone of a portable radio?	☐	☐	☐
3) If you wanted to hear someone's heartbeat, which ear would you place against their chest?	☐	☐	☐
4) Imagine a small box resting on a table. This box contains a small clock. Which ear would you press against the box to find out if the clock was ticking?	☐	☐	☐
Totals:	☐	☐	☐

Eyedness Questionnaire

	Left	Right	Either
1) Which eye would you use to look through a telescope?	☐	☐	☐
2) If you had to look into a dark bottle to see how full it was, which eye would you use?	☐	☐	☐
3) Which eye would you use to look through a key-hole?	☐	☐	☐
4 Which eye would you use to sight down a rifle?	☐	☐	☐
Totals:	☐	☐	☐

Interpretation of Questionnaires

Use the scoring method as shown for hands on page 101, but use the table below to interpret the findings for each of the above tests:

Score	Result
11 - 12	strongly right-sided.
9 - 10	mixed right-sided.
8	ambi-sided.
6 - 7	mixed left-sided.
4 - 5	strongly left-sided.

Body Language

Body language actions, such as hand clasping, arm crossing and leg crossing are genetically controlled actions and they are not linked to handedness. They tend to run in families.

When clasping hands, either the left or right thumb is placed on top. It is equally common for right-handers as left-handers to place their left thumb on top. When folding arms, those who fold the left wrist on top of the right are not necessarily consistent with their direction when clasping hands, nor does it relate to their handedness. When sitting and crossing one leg over the other, about 66 per cent of the population cross the right over the left leg, regardless of their handedness. [9]

Obviously, professional researchers have access to scientific information which school and college pupils do not. Nor do the latter have the funding, qualifications or expertise to produce such in-depth, controlled experiments. Their projects are on a much less sophisticated level and, as many students simply do not know where or how to begin, some basic suggestions are given here which may help them get started.

GUIDELINES 8

1) If you wish to conduct a small scale survey, using questionnaires in a school, or schools, you will need first of all to obtain permission from the head teacher(s). The anonymity of the school, teachers and pupils should be assured. You may wish to try a different questionnaire on parents. Small samples are unlikely to produce very accurate results. For a larger survey, however, you might need to discuss your intentions with parent and teacher associations, school governors, or teacher unions.

2) When attempting a test, or questionnaire, it must be done two or three times, in case variations are shown.

3) Different types of assessments should also be tried, to see if results differ.

4) If you are drawing up your own questionnaire, watch for ambiguities and leading questions. One survey asked parents to fill in a form for their child. Asked first for name, age and sex, many of them filled in their own details instead of the child's, completely ruining the entire survey. Questionnaires should be short and concise to avoid discouraging participants. Try your model out first on colleagues, then make adjustments rather than finding out after the survey that it was inadequate.

5) Some criteria to look for: a) direction of handedness; b) degree of handedness; c) ratio of left- to right-handed pupils; d) ages; e) sex differences; f) ratio of left- to right-handed teachers; g) awareness of teachers to left-handers in classes; h) provision of seating, equipment, help, etc.; i) handedness of relatives.

6) Visit your main reference library and ask the librarian to make a search for appropriate abstracts, indexes, books. Look in British Books in Print and The British National Bibliography for left-handed titles. ASLIB is an index to theses accepted for higher degrees in British Universities. Abstracts to theses are on microfiche. The British Library Lending Division holds reports, translations and theses. Try the sections on psychology, education, special educational needs, handwriting, medicine, neurology. Look at appropriate periodicals as well as books. Some college and certainly university libraries will have copies of research papers or will obtain them for you.

7) If you wish to find some testimonials, for example, from older left-handers who may have been forced to change or punished, children experiencing particular difficulties, etc., try writing to the readers' letters column of your weekly and regional daily newspaper. If you want to spread your net further, you could write to several around the country. Depending on the aspect you are studying, you could also write to specialist magazines, such as women's or parenting magazines, and educational, trade or professional magazines. You will find addresses in the library in PIMS, the PR Planner, Willing's Press Guide or Benn's Newspaper Press Directory. Write to editorial, not advertising offices.

8) Read newspaper cuttings of articles on left-handedness. Your regional daily paper may have a library you can consult. The Daily Telegraph has a library you may be able to use. Press cuttings agency charges would be prohibitive. The British Museum Newspaper Library Reading Room is at Colindale, London.

9) Caution should be taken in repeating facts from the popular press as most journalists know little about the subject and their sources are not stated. Their job is to report on information given to them, which they accept in good faith, and they have no way – and generally, no time – to verify facts. Consequently, quite a lot of nonsense has been printed on the subject, mostly of a frivolous nature, which has become 'folklore' and is often repeated elsewhere. Also, some writers sensationalise aspects of new research, often taking it out of context. Most scientific writers or responsible feature writers for parenting or medical publications, for example, can usually be relied upon, mainly because they have more time to do their research thoroughly, check their facts and apply to authentic sources for their information.

10) When stating facts in a report remember to give your source of information. It shows that you have not made them up, helps others who might want to refer to the documents, and is a matter of courtesy to the originator.

11) Reference libraries will usually have reference books giving addresses of agents for personalities, sporting organisations, and professional and trade associations. MPs can be contacted direct at the House of Commons or Lords. The University of Loughborough has an ergonomics research department. Laterality researchers can be contacted at the psychology departments of their universities. Always enclose a stamped, addressed envelope when writing to anyone for information.

Footnotes:

1   Bishop, Dorothy. *Handedness and Development Disorder* (London: Erlbaum, 1990).

2   Coren, S. *Left-Hander* (London: John Murray, 1993).

3   Oldfield, R. C. *The assessment and analysis of handedness: The Edinburgh Inventory* (Neuropsychologia, 19, 1971). Pages 97-114.

4   McManus, I. C., B. Murray, K. Doyle and S. Baron-Cohen. *Handedness in childhood autism shows a dissociation of skill and preference* (Cortex, 28, 1992). Pages 373-381.

5   Soper, H. V., P. Satz, D. L. Orsini, W. G. Van Gorp and M. F. Green. *Handedness distribution in a residential population with severe or profound mental retardation* (American Journal of Mental Deficiency, 92, 1987). Pages 94-102.

6   Annett, M. *The growth of manual preference and speed* (British Journal of Psychology, 61, 1970a). Pages 545-558.

7   Annett, M. and M. Manning. *The disadvantages of dextrality for intelligence* (British Journal of Psychology, 80, 1989). Pages 213-226. Also Annett, M. and M. Manning. *Reading and a balanced polymorphism for laterality and ability* (Journal of Child Psychology, Psychiatry, 31, 1990). Pages 511-529.
Annett, M. *Left, Right, Hand and Brain: the Right Shift Theory* (Hillsdale: Erlbaum, 1985).

8   Porac, C. and S. Coren. *The dominant eye* (Psychological Bulletin, 83, 1976). Pages 880-897.

9   Blau, A. *The Dominant Hand* (Research Monograph, No. 5, American Orthopsychiatric Association, New York, 1946).

11 INFORMATION SOURCES

Further Reading

Alston, J. *Writing Left-Handed* (Manchester: Dextral Books, 1996).

Annett, M. *Left, Right, Hand and Brain: the Right Shift Theory* (Hillsdale: Erlbaum, 1985).

Bell, J. *Doing Your Research Project – a guide for first-time researchers in education and social science* (Milton Keynes: Open University Press, 1991).

Bishop, D. V. M. *Handedness and Developmental Disorder* (London: Erlbaum, 1990).

Blakeslee, T. *The Right Brain* (London: Macmillan, 1980).

CLHS. *Laterality Report* (Manchester: CLHS, 1992).

Coren, S. *Left-Hander* (London: John Murray, 1993).

Hornsby, B. *Overcoming Dyslexia – A Straightforward Guide for Families and Teachers* (London: Vermilion, 1997).

Nash-Wortham, M. and J. Hunt. *Take Time* (Stourbridge: The Robinswood Press, 1997).

Paul, D. *Living Left-Handed* (London: Bloomsbury, 1997).

Pollock, J. and E. Waller. *Day-to-Day Dyslexia in the Classroom* (London: Routledge, 1997).

Quinn, V., and A. MacAuslan. *Dyslexia – What Parents Ought to Know* (London: Penguin, 1997).

Sassoon, R. *Handwriting: The Way to Teach it* and *Handwriting: A New Perspective* (Cheltenham: Leopard Learning, 1995).

Sassoon, R. *The Art and Science of Handwriting* (Oxford: Intellect, 1993).

Serfontein, Dr. G. *The Hidden Handicap – how to help children who suffer from dyslexia, hyperactivity and learning difficulties* (Australia: Simon and Schuster, 1996).

Springer and Deutsch. *Left Brain, Right Brain* (New York: WH Freeman, 5th edition, 1997).

Studley, V. *Left-Handed Calligraphy* (New York: Van Nostrand Reinhold, 1979; reprinted New York: Dover Publications, 1991).

NFER. *Helping Left-Handed Children* (Slough: NFER-Nelson, *Topic* Issue 14, Autumn, 1994).

New Zealand Council for Educational Research. *Helping Left-Handed Children* (Wellington: Set One 1997).

Wallis Myers, P. *The Handwriting Manual* (1996).

Welchman, M. and J. *Suggestions for Helping the Dyslexic Child in the Classroom* (Bath: Better Books, 1981).

Previous Guidelines for Left-handed Children

Clark, M. M. *Teaching Left-Handed Children* (Sevenoaks: Hodder and Stoughton, 1974).

Cole, L. *Instruction in Penmanship for the Left-Handed Child* (*Elementary School Journal*, 39, 1939). Pages 436-48.

Gardner, W. H. *Left-handed Writing – Instruction Manual* (Danville, Illinois: The Interstate Company, 1945).

Useful Addresses

Advisory Centre for Education (ACE).
lb Aberdeen Studios, 22 Highbury Grove, London N5 2EA   (020 7354 8321)

Association of Educational Psychologists.
26 The Avenue, Durham DH1 4ED   (0191 384 9512)

British Dyslexia Association. *(Information Centre)*
98 London Road, Reading, Berkshire RGl 5AU   (0118 966 8271)

British Orthoptic Society.
Tavistock House Nth, Tavistock Sq., London WC1H 9HX   (020 7387 7992)

Dyslexia Institute.
133 Gresham Road, Staines, Middlesex TW18 2AJ   (01784 459498)

Dyspraxia Foundation.
8 West Alley, Hitchin, Herts SG5 lEG   (01462 454986)

International Hornsby Centre. *(Dyslexia teacher training centre.)*
Glenshee Lodge, 261 Trinity Road, London SW18 3SN   (020 8874 1844)

LADDER. *(A.D.D.)*
PO Box 700, Wolverhampton WV3 7YY

National Foundation for Educational Research. (NFER)
The Mere, Upton Park, Slough, Berkshire SL1 2DQ   (01753 574123)

Parent's Charter Unit, Department for Education.
Sanctuary Buildings, Great Smith Street, Westminster, London SWlP 3BT

Professional Association of Teachers of Students
with Specific Learning Difficulties. (PATOSS)
PO Box 66, Cheltenham, Gloucestershire GL53 9YF

Recommended Suppliers of Left-handed Goods

Allt for vansterhanta.
Box 8812, 402 71, Göteborg, Sweden   (0031 55 64 01)

Anything Left-Handed. *(Shops and mail order.)*
Head Office and Enquiries:
18 Avenue Road, Belmont, Surrey SM2 6JD   (020 8770 3722)
www.anythingleft-handed.co.uk
Shops:
57 Brewer Street, London WR1 3FB   (020 7437 3910)
14 Norfolk Avenue, Christchurch, Dorset BH23 2SE   (01202 484013)
21 Pallister Road, Clacton-on-Sea, Essex CO15 1PQ   (01255 479004)
5 Charles Street, Worcester WR1 2AQ   (01905 25798)

Peter Cook's Guitar World.
69 Station Road, Hanwell, London W7 3JD   (020 8840 1244)

Disabled Living Foundation. *(Music for left hands.)*
380-384 Harrow Road, London W9 2HU   (020 7289 6110)
National Help-line   (0845 130 9177)
Textphone   (020 7432 8009)

Dr Tree U KG.
Neubaugasse, 1070, Vienna, Austria

The Keyboard Company. *(Computer keyboards.)*
8 Canal Ironworks, Hope Hills, London Road,
Brimscombe, Stroud, Glos. GL5 2SH   (07000-102105)

La Main Gauche. *(Shop and mail order.)*
BP75-69564 St Genis Laval, Cedex, France   (0033 72 39 36 14)

The Left Centre at The Old Police Station. *(Shop.)*
57 Waterloo Street, Ironbridge, Shrops TF8 7AA   (01952 433838)

Lefthanded Products Ltd.
P.O. Box 2060, Raumati Beach 6450, New Zealand

Left-Handers International.
PO Box 8249, Topeka, Kansas 66608 U.S.A

Left-Handed Products.
81 George Street, The Rocks, Sydney 2000, Australia

Left Hand World. *(Shop.)*
PO Box 39 P-8B, San Francisco,
California 94133, U.S.A.   (001 415 433 3547)

Lefty Products.
PO Box 91821, West Vancouver, BC, Canada

Professional Music Technology Ltd. *(Left-handed guitars and basses.)*
136 Lawley Middleway, Birmingham.   (0121 359 5056)

PCD Maltron Ltd. *(Specialist computer keyboards.)*
15 Orchard Lane, East Molesey, Surrey KT8 0BN   (020 8398 3265)

Route 66 Guitars.
1507 North Gardner Street, Hollywood,
California 90046 U.S.A.   (001 213 850 6331)

Godfrey Syrett Ltd. *(Left-handed desk rests.)*
Planet Place, Killingworth,
Newcastle-upon-Tyne NE12 6DY   (0191 268 1010)

For other titles from The Robinswood Press, contact
www.robinswoodpress.com